VLT,

The White Tortilla

May you always aspire to "dream big dreams," and achieve them.

Best wishes,

[signature]

D0721789

Sept 2005

The White Tortilla:
Reflections of a Second-Generation
Mexican-American

David P. Diaz, Ed.D.
Atascadero, 2005

The White Tortilla: Reflections of a Second-Generation Mexican-American.

Revised version with reading guide, January 2005.
0-9755763-2-1
Copyright© 2004, 2005 by David P. Diaz.

All rights reserved. No part of this book can be reproduced in any form or by any means, electronic or mechanical, including photocopying, recording or by any information storage and retrieval system, without the expressed written permission of the author.

Many parts of this book are fiction. Any reference to historical events, to real people, living or dead, is intended to embellish the narrative events of this book. Most names and characters in this book are used fictitiously and their resemblance, if any, to real life counterparts is often, but not always, coincidental.

Please visit The White Tortilla web site at:
http://www.thewhitetortilla.com

To my children Christina, Valerie, Paul David and Gabriella—I hope that the lessons of The White Tortilla bring you some measure of success and happiness. I encourage you to always aspire to "dream big dreams" and to pursue those dreams with all the passion you can muster.

"I'm a great believer in luck, and I find the harder I work, the more I have of it." ~ Thomas Jefferson

"Adversity causes some men to break; others to break records." ~ William A. Ward

"Let the beauty of who you are be what you do." ~ Rumi

Contents

Acknowledgements

I would like to thank the following people who graciously provided their expertise to make this book a reality. Thanks to Ed Conklin, Francisco Curiel, Jennifer O'Brien, Thomas Newman, Walt Rehm, Bill Wesnousky and Jennifer Wesnousky for reading the manuscript and for providing key suggestions. I cannot express just how valuable your comments were in completing this book.

Also to my wife—who reads everything I write—for reading the manuscript several times and for enduring my constant requests for "help!"

Thanks to my daughter Christina, for inspiring me and encouraging me to complete this book.

Introduction

I'll start by saying that, although I hadn't heard the phrase until just recently, I share the experience of "The White Tortilla." As the eldest daughter of the author (whom I like to call 'Dad'), I have experienced years of ethnic ambiguity.

It began at the basic level of filling out college applications, SAT's, insurance forms, and numerous other questionnaires that ask you to classify your race or ethnicity. Simply put, if you've got a #2 pencil and a form in your hand, people wanna know *who you are.*

For me, the question is always the same: which box do I check? Mexican? Hispanic? Of Hispanic origin or descent?

Or is it Caucasian, White, or not of Hispanic descent or origin?

I like to call myself one-third Mexican, but is that really true? If I'm not over 50% of any race or nationality does that mean I'm just a mutt? Would I be lying to say I am "not of Hispanic decent," if any part of me is?

I usually give up trying to "define myself" and end up checking Mexican half the time and Caucasian the other half. Who knows who really keeps track of these things? How many people really care?

With a last name like Diaz, people tend to make some assumptions about who I am. As an actor, a Mexican surname on my resume means that before directors turn over my "head-shot" or hear a "pitch" from my agent, they envision long, dark hair, chestnut eyes, olive skin: an ethnic beauty. Quite a surprise when they get me. I look at my family pictures and wonder where my blonde hair and blue eyes came from. With my dad's black hair and brown eyes and mom's brown hair and green eyes, I usually become the brunt of harmless jokes—the "mailman's daughter." Was it my mom's Spanish side coming out or was it her Irish side? Or was it really the "Arrowhead water guy"?

When I tell people that "Diaz" is a Mexican name they assume I know Spanish—ask me where in Mexico my family is from. Four years in High School didn't make me fluent and . . . no, I still can't remember where my grandfather came from.

How many of my dad's Mexican traits were passed down to me, to my brother, my sister? We all have similar features, but our coloring couldn't be more different. All we know is that we are three people who come from a split family where one side has ham and turkey for Christmas dinner and the other side tamales and chiles rellenos. *Comprende*?

My dad has always motivated us children to work hard, study smart, dream big, and make something for ourselves. I purposely say make something *for* and not *of* ourselves, because dad already knows the potential that we possess, he just wants us to create a future that will live up to that potential.

Sometimes we'd balk, sulk, say he was lecturing us (acting like the teacher that he is), and refuse to listen. In fact, every time I go home to visit, my dad reminds me that grad school is waiting for me; that I could do so well, if I went back. It's probably true; I would do well, yet he very much supports my career as an actor.

Having a good education is very important; being successful is important—I admire that in my dad. It's his desire to strive for "greater things" that has been passed down to me. I think my mother's sense of joy and quest for happiness, together with my dad's perfectionism and drive to achieve, make for a very exciting and promising mix in myself as an actor.

There was so much I didn't know about my dad and his family—a fact blatantly evident when I sat down to read this book. I didn't look up until I was finished; it was past two in the morning and my eyes were aching, but I didn't care. It was probably more than I had learned about *mi familia* in almost 26 years. It was enlightening, to say the least.

I was fascinated to learn of my dad's origins and to put into perspective the lessons he has taught us. I can only imagine how those traits might some day be passed down to the forth- and fifth-generation Mexican-Americans who follow me.

Christina Marie Diaz

Chapter 1
The White Tortilla

"We must learn to live together as brothers or perish together as fools." ~ Martin Luther King Jr.

"Hey *pocho*. Don't look at me *pendejo* or I'll slap that look off your face." That was Butchie Gonzalez; I hated him. Butchie was a fat, greasy "beaner," whose hair was slicked back with a handful of "Butch Wax," hence the name, I suppose. He wore baggy, *pachuco*[1] pants and black shoes with toes so pointy that they could be used for ice picks. He said he wore them in case he got in a fight, and he got in plenty. His pants were old and had patches sewn over patches, and his shoes were well worn but shined with plenty of black shoe polish.

My friends called Butchie *El Indio*[2] (The Indian) because he was so dark. I called him a lot worse, but since my Catholic faith demanded several Our Fathers and Hail Marys for cuss words, I usually just stuck with *El Indio*, though not to his face of course.

Butchie's vocabulary was lethal—he had trouble stringing together more than two or three non-cusswords. He apparently had a lot of grief to purge. I never saw him in a good mood. He seemed profoundly disturbed by every aspect of his life and he took it out on those around him, especially me. His being a poor, fat beaner was a heavy cross to bear, I guess. Butchie only fit in with the *pachucos* of the world, those who could tolerate one another only through common dress, language, and demeanor.

One thing about Butchie though, that boy could dance. He was the best I ever saw at the "Twist" or the "Mashed Potatoes," or whatever other new dance craze was around. I was always too shy to dance, but I could watch Butchie forever. He would put a 45 on his tiny, beat-up record player and grind those black shoes into the floor and sweat grease out of his dark pores. He would grab his younger sister and twirl her back and forth, it was the only time he ever put a smile on his face. My guess is that the term "cutting the rug" must've come from someone watching Butchie dancing with his pointy black shoes.

Butchie and his two best friends liked to call themselves "*Los Tres Reyes*." The Three Kings indeed, more like the three stooges, if you ask me. These wannabe "gangbangers" were so pitiful that they couldn't even find a proper gang to belong to and had to make up their own.

The only two topics of conversation that occupied this triumvirate brain trust were fighting and "girls."

They would wait down on the corner of Ponoma and 5th streets every afternoon and call out to the girls walking home from school.

On this afternoon, Butchie puffed out his chest and gesticulated—calling out to Lupe Valdez as she walked toward the group. "Hey *mamuchis. ¡Cúrame mamacita!*" said Butchie as she drew closer.

She crossed the street to put some distance between her and *Los Tres Reyes*, then she flipped them all "the bird" and picked up her pace.

"*Hijole*," said "Squeeky" Garcia, one of *Los Tres*. "She's a mean one, but sexy, she reminds me of your sister," he teased Butchie.

"*¡Tu madre!*" said Butchie in retort.

"*¡No me molestas, ese!*" said Squeeky as he started to "pimp" and bounce around like he wanted to fight.

Butchie sneered, trying hard not to laugh. "Okay *chingón. Olvídalo.* Let's go back to my place, nothin's happening here."

Butchie and his friends were 3 or 4 years older than me. I was shy and didn't have many friends and I liked hanging out with the older guys in the neighborhood.

Today, as usual, I was tagging along with *Los Tres*, albeit at a casual distance. Butchie didn't mind having me around if he was alone, but when he was with friends, he started in on me.

"Stupid *pocho*. Get outta here *baboso*, go play with my sister, she's in the backyard."

Sister Linda (pronounced "sees-ter Lean-duh") was tall and skinny, and just as dark as

9

Butchie. She wore plain sackcloth dresses with flowers sewn on that her mom made her. I didn't like her either, but at least she was quiet and didn't pick on me like Butchie.

I don't know why he called me such names. I didn't know what *pocho* meant at the time, and I never asked my parents because I figured it was just one of the many cuss words that Butchie infused into his well-practiced repertoire and that, if I even mentioned it around my mother I would have my mouth washed out with soap. Again. Though I was no stranger to the soap-in-the-mouth treatment, I was a quick learner and became a model citizen while within earshot of my parents. Together, the Our Father's and Hail Mary's—offered in repentance—along with a liberal dose of soap, became my guides on the road to sanctity.

"I don't wanna play with Linda, I wanna hang out with you guys," I complained.

"¡*Chupa mis huevos*, you little *culo!*" Butchie spat. I had had enough abuse for one day and so I left his house and went back down the street to our store.

Pocho is a term that is often used to describe Mexicans that have lost, or given up, their heritage. And yet, as far as I knew, I hadn't lost nor given up anything. I was just struggling to survive like everyone else in Oxnard, trying to make friends in an ethnically rich (read: volatile) neighborhood and trying to make it through school everyday without incurring a death penalty from God—as meted out by the nuns. I had plenty on my mind for a 10-year-old.

I found it more than frustrating that my Mexican friends treated me as "white" and my white friends treated me as "Mexican." I felt like I was in a limbo of ethnic identity: one foot in the Mexican culture and the other foot in the white majority camp. In short, I just didn't fit in. I did not possess, as it were, enough of the requisite characteristics for authentic "membership" in any group.

When in the company of my white friends, I became the brunt of every new "beaner" joke. "Why can't Mexicans barbecue? Because the beans keep falling through the grill." This and countless other jokes (*ad infinitum, ad nauseum*)—as well as ignorant stereotypes (e.g., "macho" or "hot-blooded" Mexican)—were intended to keep me "in my place" and were a way to elevate the status of the joker and lower my status proportionately. Conversely, my Mexican friends would call me "whitey," "*blanco*," or "*pocho*." Though these taunts were not, most often, intentionally malignant, they hurt and they had the effect of reminding me of my status as an outsider. A few years later, one Mexican woman would use the term "The White Tortilla" to describe my persona. The term stuck and I became "*La Tortilla Blanca*," to the amusement of my friends who liked the sound of it. The feminine form of the noun was not wasted on them as a double entendre.

***

It's ironic that a White Tortilla like myself would have any trouble fitting in to the

American societal majority. My parents instilled in me the desire to accept and embrace the ideals and practices of all cultures and to utilize any of those strengths that would help me to achieve my goals and dreams.

In my estimation, the term "White Tortilla" aptly describes an admixture of characteristics that include elements from the culture of ones ancestors as well as the culture(s) where one's family has been transplanted. The traits that emerge often reveal a strong and resilient character and can form the basis of ones success.

As family generations move further and further from the native transplants that immigrated from their country of origin, they continually mix elements of their native culture with elements of the other cultures with which they interact. At some point this integration reaches critical mass and a common identity emerges. This is true diversity, in my opinion. Not just the existence of apparent differences, but also the melding of customs, traditions, beliefs and practices into a strong and unified whole.

A major obstacle, however, is that many people will not allow change to happen. Instead of recognizing and accepting the changes wrought by diversity as a normal evolution toward assimilation, acceptance, and a common culture, many will instead use change as a springboard to discrimination, stereotyping and bigotry.

I use the metaphor of basket weaving to illustrate how a White Tortilla embodies true diversity. In Spanish, the words "la canasta" refer to a basket—one that is woven from many individual threads. Threads of different colors and variations, blended together into a cohesive whole. As a whole, the woven threads consist of something that is as beautiful and strong as it is useful. The completed basket is congealed into a resilient unity—holistic, with strength of purpose and function. When separated from the whole, the individual strands possess uniqueness, but lack meaning and purpose and represent utility and success only in their potential.

I now use the term, "White Tortilla," with pride, as an icon representing true diversity in America. The term engenders in second generation Americans, of any ethnicity, similar beliefs and practices probably taught by their parents, which were intended to lead to success.

First generation Americans wanted to be successful in America and developed a set of "how-to's" or rules for success. Two of the common features transmitted by parents to their children were a desire to assimilate into the dominant culture and a determination to obtain the best education possible. Ideally, these tendencies create a paradigm for success, a strategy for adapting to the challenges of the modern world.

For many second generation Americans, however, it hasn't turned out quite as expected. Many who have followed this path are unaware of the richness of their native culture. It's not that they have "lost" their culture, but rather, ironically, they have had their cultural traits inadvertently, yet systematically, displaced by the philosophies of their own parents who believed that they could help ensure their children's success. In other words, many of the White Tortillas of the world are living out a blueprint for life designed by those who love them and are interested in their health, happiness and success. Yet, by choosing this lifestyle, they often get caught in a purgatory of ambivalence: too white to represent their native culture and too native to represent the majority.

While still an undergraduate, I was approached by some well-meaning Latinos to become a part of the *Movimiento Estudiantil Chicano de Aztlán* (MEChA) organization. According to the Philosophy Papers, MEChA "is a student organization that promotes higher education, cultura, and historia."[3] MEChA student groups sponsor social events, conduct meetings, and members often attend conferences.

Jesús was in my speech class. He was a gregarious Mexican with a huge smile, a potbelly and an infectious laugh. He was some kind of officer in the campus MEChA organization and so he was especially concerned with my poor *pocho* soul. He kept pestering me about getting involved, to get "in touch" with my Chicano-ness, I guess. I went to several meetings but felt a strange sense of angst, suffering all these people speaking in a "foreign" tongue and promoting the gospel of ethnic pride. I simply never quite got it. What was all the fuss about being Mexican? Weren't we all Americans? Would all this ethnocentric activity help me become successful? Would this extracurricular ethnicity-building get the attention of the affirmative action cops and translate into success? Not according to the dogma preached by my parents. There were no free rides—assimilation was essential in their view. Not assimilation in the same sense that a chameleon or butterfly can blend into their surroundings and not be noticed by predators. But, rather, like athletes that have so honed their innate abilities so as to be recognized and rewarded for their efforts. In other words, contrary to the idea of conformity to some perceived status quo, assimilation meant *distinguishing* one's self in a positive and mutually beneficial way.

As an undergraduate at Cal Poly, I was awarded an educational grant from the Spanish American Institute (SAI) of Los Angeles. I was sponsored for this grant by one of my father's Latino friends. I really didn't know anything about the organization except that they gave me several hundred dollars to attend college, and for that I was grateful. It was understandable that, upon graduating, SAI would ask me to appear at one of their conferences to make a presentation. In fact, since I listed guitar playing as one of my hobbies, they asked if I would perform a guitar number. Though not too excited about performing, I talked a friend of mine into playing with me in front of a crowd of over 500 Latinos. How naïve I was at the time, to not even consider that an organization such as SAI was looking for presentations that would uplift the Latino culture—it never even occurred to me. I still remember playing and singing a 1970's pop/gospel song to about 500 blank faces. When I was finished, I walked determinedly through a gauntlet of stunned

Latinos and not one of those 500 souls could so much as utter their condolences.

I am a White Tortilla. At first through indoctrination, and later deliberately, I have decided to follow the educational and cultural philosophies of my first-generation parents. Though my practices of these ideals are different in many cases, I share the same ideals: I have been taught, and have accordingly taught my children, to be assimilators—to so highly develop their academic, language and cultural skills as to be distinguished in all that they do. I have also taught them to live with the high expectations of a level playing field and to develop intimate relationships with all people, treating others with respect, regardless of their status or position. This is my story, and it may be yours.

Chapter 2
A "Good Education"

"Excellence is the best deterrent to racism—therefore be excellent." ~ Jessie Jackson

It was after school and my mom was working the cash register and my dad was behind the meat counter cutting up chickens. We owned a market at that time called—simply enough—Diaz Market. It was a "mom and pop" grocery store that represented the culmination of my parents' efforts at success in America. I learned many things in that store—how to stock shelves, clean and stack produce, and how to check and bag groceries—pretty much everything except how to cut up a chicken. My dad was a butcher by trade and I watched him break and bone hundreds, maybe thousands of chickens. You would think that I would've learned to cut meat by osmosis or something. To this day, I couldn't cut up a chicken if my life depended on it.

"*Mi hijo*, what are you up to?" said my father as I walked up to the butcher block. My mind was still parsing one of Butchie's daily diatribes and I wondered if I should ask my dad about *pocho*.

"Nothing, I stayed late at school today and then went to Butchie's house," I said as I watched his knife carve effortlessly around the gristle. No sense in bothering him with such blubber.

I watched as he worked, noticing as always his perfect attire for his job. He wore a clean and heavily starched white shirt with a bow tie, dark green "CHP" pants, heavy black leather belt and black "Frye" boots. Of course, as a butcher, he topped off his ensemble with a long white smock. That's all he wore, ever. His closet was a study in cloning, all those white shirts, green pants and the same black boots for every occasion. Nothing changed. He was a creature of habit, craving the comfort afforded by the mundane.

As he used the cleaver to break yet another chicken back, I looked at his hands. My dad had the softest hands for someone who worked so hard. It was from years of handling meat, he said. All that fat and grease coated his hands and acted like some kind of hand lotion. He loved working that store, but still, that wasn't what he wanted for his kids.

"What did you learn in school today *mi'jo*?[4] Did you study hard? Remember to study hard and learn good, I don't want you to cut chickens and haul beef the rest of your life."

My parents both preached the gospel of education. I guess they figured a 9th grade education, like their own, would buy only Diaz Market, not Wal-Mart. They continually told us that a good education would ensure us a first-rate, steady job, one where we wouldn't have to work so hard and long. They wanted a "better life"—whatever that meant—for their kids and they figured an education had some correlation. I wasn't so sure about that at the time, but discipline made me impressionable.

"Dad, why do I have to go to Catholic school? The nuns are mean and I am always afraid that my answers will be wrong."

Actually, I wasn't *just* afraid to be wrong, I was also often afraid to be right. It was many years later before I would grasp the reality that the fear of success is every bit as paralyzing as the fear of failure. Success is the escort of further achievement and change, both of which can be unsettling to the insecure. Punishment for failure in school was severe in those days—ruler slaps across the backs of the hands, ear-twisting and old-fashioned tongue-lashings were the norm. Further, for shy kids like myself, being the center of attention as an example to others was a constant dread. So, I kept quiet as much as possible, no doubt stunting my own intellectual curiosity and growth.

Unsurprisingly, my school had its proverbial "Sister Mary Pain." Squared. Actually, we called her Super Sister, because though she was a frail looking, pasty-faced woman, she was faster than a speeding cuss word and would leap on tall children in a single bound.

She had embarrassed me the week before. We wore the uniforms characteristic of Catholic school, which were part and parcel of the assembly line of godliness, I guess. But, once a month, we could wear other "acceptable" uniforms, such as Boy Scout, Cub Scout, Girl Scout, etc. I wore my Cub Scout uniform for the very first and, as it turned out, last time on that day. I was talking with a friend who wanted to know something about the patches on my uniform when up walked the sister and grabbed me by my gold and blue neckerchief. She pulled me up until my toes were just barely touching the ground. Up, up, up, to the front of the class. I was the sacrificial lamb of the day, ordained to teach others the penalty of crossing the boundaries of good sense, or whatever. To this day I still wonder what I did to deserve that chastening.

"I don't know," said my father. "We are Catholic and your school is part of our religion *mi'jo*. And besides, Catholic school provides the best education and you know how important that is. Your mother and I pay for you to go to that school so you will be more educated than us and so you won't have to work so hard like we have. Maybe I will go with you and talk with the sisters. Straighten everything out."

"No, that's okay dad. Forget it, really, I'll be alright." I could just imagine how that would play out.

I always felt bad at times like these. I didn't like to disappoint my dad; he had such high hopes for me, and yet, I hated the gut-wrenching fear inspired by the daily alter call for the wicked. These daily trials and other indignities foisted upon us sinners created a sense of dread that impeded my ability to learn. In the end, I didn't last long in Catholic school, my First Holy Communion, which marked my "separation unto God," also marked the beginning of my separation from His church.

In another type of separation, Diaz Market wasn't destined to succeed. The government bought our store at a price of their asking because they felt the need to expand the Port of Hueneme. They soon turned that property into a shipyard. After 16 years of business, my parents had to close their doors and my father was separated from his dream of independence and forced to return to a workforce that he had never made peace with in the past. That was the beginning of the last chapter in my father's life, a sad and downward spiral of compromise and capitulation.

***

According to my parents, success required getting a good education, and that meant not only attending Catholic school, but also attending college. Since my parents had completed at least some secondary education, they must have figured that the magic elixir of success was to be found beyond high school. Thus, my destiny was to be forged in a post-secondary education.

In fact, I never really doubted that I would someday attend college. I had heard it so much during my youth that I never considered not going. At about 12 years of age, in response to my mother's question, "Are you going to go to college?" I responded, "Doesn't everybody?"

However, attending college was an abstract concept. With no role models in my family, I never really understood what "going to college" really entailed. I knew that I would enroll; I just didn't know what I was supposed to do once I got there.

I still remember the day that I was applying for admission to Cal Poly State University in San Luis Obispo, California. The counselor at my junior college said that I must declare a major. That concept chilled me to the bone and I was totally unprepared for such an undertaking. I was "going to college," wasn't that sufficient? What was this new thing called "declaring a major?" The discussion went something like this:

Counselor: "Mister Diaz, I have read over your application. Everything looks fine except that you must declare a major."

"A what?" I stammered.

"A major, you have to declare a major."

"Oh, okay. What do you think I should pick?" I said, feeling a bit flustered.

"Well, that's something I can't decide for you," he said in his most official-sounding voice. "You have to choose something that you find interesting. Can you tell me what you are interested in?"

"How about basketball or tennis?" I ventured, not sounding altogether convincing.

And so it was that I declared a major. Physical Education would be my chosen field, not because I knew anything about the academics involved or the job markets that would be open to me, but because I had played sports from the time I was young and could think of nothing else I might be more interested in. Though I feel quite fortunate to have chosen Physical Education as my discipline, I've always wondered that if I'd had some family member or friend as a role model in the educational arena, if I would have gone in a different direction.

After five and a half years, I finally graduated with a Bachelor's degree in Physical Education, the delay probably due to academic indifference—I was more interested in sports and "girls" than academics.

I thought I was done with college after completing one degree. I had achieved a major goal, decreed by my parents to guarantee success—the purported birthright of those metamorphosed by education. Except for one minor detail. I still didn't know what I wanted to be when I "grew up."

Just what does one do with a B.S. in P.E.? If I wanted to teach, I would need to pursue a teaching credential or a Master's Degree, depending on what level I wished to teach.

Since I had traversed my education without an idea of what I wanted to accomplish with my degree, I was at a loss for what to do with my life at that point. This is a common curse of poor academic planning and underachievement, regardless of the academic discipline.

The problem was that I followed my parent's philosophy of assimilation only incompletely: though I distinguished myself in sport, I didn't yet have the same focus in academics. I would not make the same mistake again.

After struggling in a purposeless void for three or four years, I decided to revisit the prescription for success, as outlined by my parents, and returned to college for yet another degree—a Master's Degree. This delighted my mother immensely, though she had absolutely no understanding of what a Master's Degree was, let alone what implications it might have to my future. Nonetheless, never wavering in her faith in "a good education," she was delighted that I had re-enlisted for another tour of duty.

Over the next several years, I divided my time between an advanced degree in Physical Education, a job and a family. I managed to secure a job at Cuesta College in San Luis Obispo as a tennis coach. Though, at that time, I didn't possess the necessary credentials to teach academic classes at the college level, I coached both men's and women's tennis teams while completing work on the M.S. degree.

This time, I pledged to throw myself completely toward my academic endeavors. At 24 years of age I actually found that I was enjoying my education more than ever. The things I was learning seemed so applicable to what I was actually doing—teaching and coaching—that I couldn't wait to finish each class so I could start another. Also, I was beginning to see the logic in a comprehensive education. College was not just something I was *going to*, but it was something that I was *taking from*. The honing of my knowledge, skills and abilities was actually contributing to my assimilation. I was becoming a marketable product, as well as a more informed participant in life. My world was becoming more exciting than it ever had been in the past.

Though it took me over six years to complete a Master's Degree (I was working 3 part time jobs), I still wasn't finished with higher education. I was obviously a glutton for punishment. After a lengthy hiatus from college—trying to distinguish myself in my career as a coach and teacher—I returned yet again to the hallowed halls of education, this time in pursuit of a doctoral degree in education.

In a doctoral program, at age 43, I was having the time of my life studying, researching, writing and rubbing elbows with others who shared my passion for learning and achievement. I threw myself delightedly toward my doctoral studies. I jumped at the chance to do whatever was necessary to distinguish myself in the program. One of my first professors in the program suggested that I should try to publish an article before writing my dissertation. He said this would help me to better understand the requirements of technical writing and research. So I did. I published not one, but six articles before I finished my doctoral program and eleven articles in the span of 4 years. In fact, I finished the doctoral program in 2 years and 7 months, 5 months earlier than the schedule and about a year and a half earlier than the norm. I also finished my dissertation in 6 months, 8 months shy of the average. This was my way of implementing my parent's definition of assimilation—distinguishing myself within the society of the majority.

One of the great injustices of life has been that my father did not live to see me complete any of my college degrees. He passed away in April of 1976, just two months before I graduated with a Bachelor's degree. Perhaps that is why I never attended any of my college commencement ceremonies. I certainly had no inherent interest in the pomp and circumstance, though I have encouraged and attended each of my children's graduation ceremonies.

My mother, who was a lesser influence on my pursuit of "a good education" early in my life, became a prime mover with a vengeance after my father died. She was my main source of support and encouragement through difficult times and times of failure.

Though my mother was very proud of my educational accomplishments, she was unable to quantify the difference between my undergraduate degree and any other. It has always been enough for her to know that I was getting "a good education" and because of that, I would succeed. To this day she never misses an opportunity to tell anyone who will listen that her son is a "Doctor of Something" and she always addresses my mail to, "Dr. David P. Diaz."

I finished my doctoral degree some twenty-four years after my father passed away; my mother was 84 years of age. I gave her a copy of my dissertation. She tried to read it but didn't finish. I didn't care; the only thing that mattered was that I dedicated it to her and my father in the preface:

To my father—whose spirit and values guide me to this day—your faith helped me to 'dream big dreams.' To my mother; many thanks; without your constant encouragement, love, and support, this would have never been possible—I share my degree with you. I love you both, and thank you from the bottom of my heart.

***

I continually encourage young people to pursue as much education as possible and to involve themselves fully in the experience. Part of a good education is to experience a wide range of activities common to a high school or collegiate life. The times spent in school are typically rich with growth, idealism and opportunities for involvement in sports, dance, theatre, the arts, clubs, and other activities, which add value and important experiences to one's life.

There is no need to rush through school to get into the workforce. The time spent working will take care of itself, it's not going anywhere and, frankly, it's not all it's cracked up to be. We will never have the opportunity to relive our high school and/or college years, so we should enjoy them while we can. By pursuing other activities besides academics during our educational stint, we demonstrate broad interests and develop an array of ancillary knowledge, skills and abilities that will make us more desirable in the marketplace.

A second reason for not rushing through school is that an education should be approached as any other important endeavor--with all the gusto one can muster. If pursuing an education, it makes sense to do it right. A broad-based general education—as well as a specialized discipline of study—will help one to dream big dreams *and* achieve them. Don't shortcut your education. Immerse yourself completely and you will be baptized in success.

The value of education cannot be underestimated or taken for granted. We not only learn the essentials of mathematics, science, history and such, but will learn to reason, assess, critically analyze and problem solve. We will also learn some of the less tangible but necessary skills of time management, organization, discipline and self-control. In sum, we will develop knowledge skills and abilities that will help us excel in many fields and aspects of life. Without a good education, we are limiting the heights to which we can dream and achieve.

Chapter 3
Finding a "Good Job"

"Be a yardstick of quality. Some people aren't used to an environment where excellence is expected." ~ Steve Jobs

Eleodoro "Leo" Velasquez was standing on the corner outside "Franco's Market," waiting for his *compadre* ("pal") Bert to get off work. Leo was a tall, skinny Mexican whose family came from Durango in Mexico.

Bert—christened Norberto Guillermo Diaz, my future father—was Leo's best friend and also from the same part of Mexico. Their parents were born and raised in Durango, Mexico, but they migrated *al norte*, finally settling in the Mexican *barrio* of El Rio, California.

Bert was learning his future trade—meat cutting—in a small market in Oxnard. "Franco's Market" was a tiny grocery store where Bert worked all parts of the store: meats, dairy, produce, frozen foods, checking, bagging and any thing else old man Franco needed. The day started about 7:00 am with opening the store, setting up the cash register, uncovering and watering the produce, and attending to myriad other tasks of operating a market. Bert started this job at age sixteen and by his eighteenth birthday was already an experienced butcher and shop keep.

He had a great desire to become successful in this country. One of five children—raised single-handedly by his mother—he quit school after finishing the 9th grade to find work and help the family survive. His own father had died at an early age and his mother never remarried, thus creating a void in the economic and emotional fabric of the family structure.

Leo too had a job, in the lemon-packing house in Oxnard. His day started and ended earlier, but was no less strenuous. Packing and hauling crates of lemons all day long was monotonous, backbreaking work, but typical of the jobs of young, uneducated (and/or poor) men and women.

"*¿Que pasó compa?*" said Leo in a gesture of familiarity and friendship.

"I'm thirsty. *Vamos a tomar,*" said Bert, tired and eager to start his weekend with a *cerveza* or two.

Having been born in the United States, the two moved easily between Spanish and English—preferring Spanish mostly for slang and short phrases.

The two walked over to a local bar—"*El Cielito Lindo*"—neither able to afford a car. They sat and talked and joked about work, friends, and what they had planned for the weekend.

The two *compadres* were going to pick up their girlfriends for a night on the town. Friday nights in the *barrio* were not much fun unless you had a car, in which case you could drive to

Ocean Park's Lick Pier and go dancing at the Aragon Ballroom. The bands of Lawrence Welk, Tommy Dorsey and others could be heard in many of the clubs of that era.

"*Oye compa*, let's go pick up Ricky and Rosie," said Leo after the two had finished washing down a week's travail with a couple of beers. "We can borrow my *tio* Memo's car tonight."

Henrietta "Ricky" Merrill was Leo's girlfriend and my future mother. (She earned her nickname through her father, who abbreviated the Spanish pronunciation of her name "Enriqueta" and called her "Ricky.") That night, the two would meet up with Ricky and Rosie at Rosie's parents house.

Sometime later that evening Leo would have to tell Ricky that he would be returning to Mexico for a while to tend to some family business. He was against the idea, but there was nothing he could do about it, Mexican family ties were strong and he could no more refuse his family's request than he could refuse to breathe.

On the way over to Rosie's, Leo was bemoaning his situation.

"*Ay tio*, I don't know what to do, I'm in love with Ricky, but I can't refuse my parents. *Oye comp*, you have to do me a favor and watch over Ricky while I'm gone."

"You know I will *compa*," said Bert, understanding well the predicament posed by family obligations.

"And you tell me if that *pendejo* Richard Perales even looks at her," said Leo with venom. "I will kick his *pinche* butt!"

Some time later, Bert would make good on his promise to watch over Ricky—he broke up with Rosie and started dating my mother. The rest, as they say, is history.

Bert and Ricky fell in love and were destined to marry. The problem was that both families initially objected to their relationship. Ricky's dad Lewis didn't approve of Bert because he was dating Rosie, and Bert's mom didn't like Ricky because she was dating . . . period. My father, eager to continue the relationship, broke up with Rosie, which resolved the one problem. However, Dominga Diaz, his mother and my future grandmother, was not so easily appeased. My grandmother did not approve of my mother because she did not observe the Mexican traditions of courtship.

Dating back to law in the 1700s, marriage couldn't take place unless all four prospective in-laws consented.[5] Often marriages were arranged whether the couple agreed or not—the parents deciding what mergers "were most beneficial to the family status and wealth." This provided an important role for the parents during the courtship period, as their approval was vital to the development of the relationship. As these rigid traditions made their way to the 20th century, they became a bit more lax, especially in the United States. Still, the practice of a lengthy and prescribed courtship, which included meeting in public places, usually in the company of the parents, was the norm.

Regardless of customs, my father was not to be deterred—he did not care much for the Mexican traditions, especially since they now lived in the United States. So, he defied my grandmother's wishes and he and my mother dated and were eventually married in Yuma, Arizona soon after their 21st birthdays. So began their 40-year union and the seed that would bring forth my two sisters and me.

As a consequence, my mother never even met my grandmother until she and my father had been married for months! This long-standing *pecado*, which I had nothing to do with, affected my parent's relationship with my grandmother and probably tainted their views of traditional Mexican cultural ideals in general.

After their nuptials, my parents initially made their home in Port Hueneme, California, living in a spare room with my mother's family. This was just temporary until the two could find good jobs and buy a house of their own.

As long as my parents lived in the *barrio*, social acceptance was a non-issue. However, outside of the *barrio*, things were different. My father waited expectantly for better things to come, but instead he learned firsthand the intolerance born of fear—fear generated by California's inexorable ethnic turnover thrust upon a hesitant and close-minded public.

When they would look for houses to rent, the common story was that my father "was too dark" and the neighbors "wouldn't approve." The problem was discrimination, a fact of life in those days and not as well disguised as today.

It seems a general characteristic of human nature to fear, hate or ridicule people who are different. Not only ethnic differences, but also in body shape and size, skin color, religion, clothes worn, evident disabilities, etc. My father was not only Mexican, but he was a dark-complected Mexican. In Mexico too, dark complexion is a curse—every country has its display of racism and intolerance. A casual survey of Mexican *telenovelas* (TV soap operas) will reveal that the heroes and heroines are light-complected and the villains, laborers and lower class people are dark. Successful politicians tend to be light-complected, and so on. Though my mother's mother was Mexican (Elena "Brina" Fernandez), my mother picked up the lighter skin of my grandfather. What a difference a couple shades of brown can make.

My father applied for many jobs that he considered to be "good jobs"—jobs with good pay, good benefits and a chance for growth and development. However, the story was always the same, nobody except for the small, independently owned businesses (and always Mexican owners), would hire him. And yet, these jobs left little room for advancement and security. He knew good jobs existed, right under his nose in fact. His white friends that he grew up with were entering the workforce in banks and department stores and in state jobs. My father was passed over, as he waited his turn in a line that seemed never to become shorter.

So, he and my mother took what jobs they could. During most of the year, my father would work in local markets cutting meat, and my mother would pack lemon crates at the packing-house in Port Hueneme.

The two of them traveled to Oregon to pick hops during the summer. Though definitely not lucrative or secure, picking hops with other itinerant laborers were times that my parents cherished. They would travel from location to location, picking hops from the early morning hours. They set up large campsites near the fields. There was music and dancing and laughter under the starry summer night skies. The food and fellowship of the evenings helped them all to digest the savagely scorching summer days of relentless stooping, picking and filling sacks with their harvest. My mother was pregnant with my oldest sister Connie at the time. She remained in camp, preparing food and readying the environment that would welcome the weary workers back from their toils.

***

After working and saving for several years—and with a loan from some well-to-do friends—my parents purchased a grocery store. "Diaz Market" and self-employment would put an end to their frustration in searching for a "good job" and permit them the modicum of success that they enjoyed for the next 16 years.

The market was small and had a tiny two-bedroom residence in the rear. My parents moved into the small living quarters with my two sisters Connie and Barbara (I would come along in another 7 years).

I inherited my work ethic at our store. From the time I could remember, I was taught any job that I could manage at my age: stocking the dairy case or food shelves, stamping prices on the canned goods, sacking groceries, or tending the produce.

What makes a job a "good job" is that it provides for some of the most basic needs: an adequate salary, benefits and security. More importantly, however, is that we must find enjoyment in our work. This is where self-employment has some advantages. There is a good feeling that comes with knowing that our efforts directly contribute to the welfare and security of the family, our loved ones. A family-owned and operated business is better yet—it extends the family experience to blend work, play, community, and discipline, through interactions between immediate family members.

Though financial security and enjoyment are important aspects within the hierarchy of needs, they will not completely satisfy our highest level of occupational needs. If we are going to last the 20 or 30 years it will take to reach retirement—and that without becoming a candidate for a padded cell—we will need a job that allows us to grow, learn and achieve. There is an innate desire for a workplace where we are respected—as we respect others—and where our ideas are taken seriously and acted upon. A good job is one that gives us a sense that we are accomplishing something meaningful with our life and is rewarding in an emotional and spiritual sense.

My father worked hard for success and waited for better things to come, but he was unable to achieve his dreams in a culture not willing to accept his service, his love and his example. Often, there is not a one-to-one correlation between hard work and success. My father was willing to do whatever it would take to achieve his dreams. His waiting eventually turned to boredom but surprisingly not bitterness, to resignation but not resentment.

***

It seems that many of today's generation are not intending to work at any job for 5 or 10 years, let alone 20 or 30. In fact, many young people change jobs as often as they change clothes—and think nothing of it.

I have considered this phenomenon at length and have decided that I am partly to blame. Having successfully assimilated as a White Tortilla, I—like many others of my kind—am now a cheerleader for change.

I have told my children how good they are since they were quite young. "You are smart. You are pretty. You can do anything you set your mind to." ("Rah, Rah, Rah!")

My youngest daughter regularly comes home from daycare with a hand painting that looks like a cross between Dali on hallucinogens and Bobo the chimp. She will bring her work up to me as I watch the news, stick it in my face and say, "Look what I did at school today!"

I hold it up to the light for a better look. First I turn it to the left, then the right and finally upside down.

"That is the best drawing I have ever seen!" I exclaim. "You are so good. What beautiful colors . . . what is it?" ("Sisk, Boom, Bah!")

My point is that somewhere along the line some of us have not effectively communicated to our children that work is . . . *work*. Sometimes things are done wrong and must be undone and redone. Or, sometimes the outcomes are merely satisfactory but could be better. By trying so hard to praise our children and positively reinforce their work at every turn, they may have missed an important distinction regarding quality, dedication and service.

It's no wonder that these same young people, upon entering the workforce, expect good jobs, high pay and excellent benefits, only to be put off by the experience of the "daily grind." They want praise and are deflated at the first bit of constructive criticism. They desire promotion, without the accompanying expectation of time served and experience gained.

A job can be exhilarating and can yield satisfaction and growth, yet we do it because we are compelled. For example, I love my job, but if I didn't have to be there, I wouldn't. I would much rather sleep in, play tennis, or write another book. Whatever else it is, work is work.

***

A White Tortilla is one who believes that there is some correlation between success in attaining a good education and success in finding a good job. A "good education" is to a "good job" as jelly is to peanut butter: without the former, it may be hard to swallow the latter. Possessing a good education qualifies us for more types of occupations, thus, increasing the probability that we will end up in a profession that meets all our criteria for a "good job."

If we have taken our education seriously, we will be well prepared for the rigors of a good job. However, if we have attempted to travel the easiest path, have expected praise, satisfaction and good grades for every effort—no matter how poor—we may find ourselves ill suited for competing at the highest level for jobs that are worthwhile.

Remember this: if we consider a job to be a "good job," others will likely consider it so as well. This creates competition. How will we rise to the top of a field of "hungry" candidates? How will we compete for jobs that are highly desirable when so many others are in the hunt too? The answer begins with our preparation. The educational process is the proving ground for success in the real world. We must begin early to make our mark. We should set our standards high and be ready to pay the price for authentic achievement.

Though having a good education doesn't *assure* us a good job, it makes it more likely. For example, completing a Master's Degree didn't earn me my current job, but it provided me the opportunity to compete. Having a

Master's Degree is a "minimum qualification" for a teaching job at the Community College level. Since all candidates must have a Master's Degree, the minimum qualification cancels itself out; this happens in many jobs. Nevertheless, it was the Master's Degree that provided me the "ticket to the show."

Ultimately, the successful candidate gets chosen, not because of their degree, but because of knowledge, skills and abilities that they have developed in the course of their educational and occupational experiences. These other deciding characteristics are demonstrated in the interviewing process.

A good education opens many doors of opportunity to a wide array of good jobs and allows options not available to those without. The White Tortilla can take advantage of this insight and walk through those doors into the vivid light beyond.

Chapter 4
The Language of Success

"Success will not lower its standard to us. We must raise our standard to success." ~ Rev. Randall R. McBride, Jr.

Education was the fountain of good fortune in the eyes of my parents. Perhaps that is why they insisted that we not learn Spanish. After all, we were in America and Americans speak English, and a good education is taught in English.

So, English became the vernacular of the Diaz household. A good education and English—written, spoken and understood perfectly—were the ideals that my parents fostered in my sisters and me.

My parents' prohibition of the Spanish language was not overt—it was a lesson that was more subliminally taught. A native speaker of Spanish, my dad would interrupt all Spanish conversations when I appeared on the scene and he, and whomever he was speaking with, would revert to English. This occurred often enough that I grew accustomed to hearing the Spanish language from afar, as an outsider. Further, it reinforced a feeling that I had developed that speaking Spanish was something to be avoided. Kind of like stealing from the "cookie jar," if you were resourceful enough to have absconded with a cookie, you kept it hidden. My parents "hid" the Spanish language purposefully.

The Spanish words spoken by my parents, their friends, and family members seemed familiar enough and even produced emotional comfort, but the meanings were not apparent. Spanish was the "muzak" of my experience, a subliminal voice, an echo of a language that I had only latent familiarity with.

My grandmother, Dominga "Minga" Diaz, was traditional to the core. She never learned to speak much English and had little patience for those who did not speak Spanish. She made an exception for me though—she loved me regardless—I was her little *pochito*. When we visited her home, she would speak in Spanish and my dad would translate for me. The only thing I remember understanding of my grandmother's speech was my name—David ("Dah-beed" as she pronounced it).

Sitting in her wheelchair (she had crippling arthritis by this time), she would stroke my head, "'Dah-beed,' que guapo tú eres. ¿Como tú Norberto, eh?"

My dad would grunt an acknowledgment: "Yes, he's handsome, but he takes after his mother in that respect."

I would sit there with my head bowed, suffering the gentle stroking of gnarled fingers across my pate—a typical encounter with *mi Abuela*. I had no interest in learning Spanish—the indoctrination of home having already set in—and was perfectly content to

42

have my dad translate for me, though I hated sitting still for such formalities. As an adult, looking back on this experience, I think this was the saddest of all my memories—I was unable to speak with my own grandmother. What a tremendous loss.

There were a few Spanish words that my parents would use interchangeably with English. Words like "*mi'jo*" (my son), or the names of certain foods (e.g., "*Nopales*"), or exclamations like, "¡*Ay Chihuahua*!" (something you might say if you burnt your finger). "¡*Vámonos*!" (Let's go!) and "¡*Ándale pronto*!" (Hurry up!) were other examples.

While I was still young, I didn't even realize that these words were not English. I mean, how could they be if English was the preferred language—the sine qua non of a good education—and my parents were speaking them? My parents had so seamlessly integrated these Spanish words into their English vocabulary that I had to learn the distinctions passively, noticing that only my Mexican friends, but not others, used these certain words.

I find it hilarious that some people think that if you don't speak Spanish you can't be a "real Mexican." I would've liked to hear someone try and explain that concept to my dad about his kids. To my parents, we were Mexican *and* American, not one or the other. The concept that all true Mexicans speak Spanish, like the belief that all "Mexicans are macho," is a stereotype—an over worn expression of bigotry that has no place in the promotion of true diversity.

***

I never really studied Spanish until after my undergraduate years. At that time, I studied voraciously both Spanish and Italian. I took the equivalent of 3 years of college-level Spanish and even traveled to the city of Cuernavaca in Mexico for an intensive course of study.

World travel, I think, helps us to productively grapple with differences between cultures and to live out situations where we are not in control. This provides an object lesson in diversity awareness and tolerance. I would recommend traveling to other countries, if only for the purpose of teaching the difficulty of communicating in a language other than one's own.

Upon arrival in Mexico for my first day of language training, the plane touched down in the airport in Mexico's capital city. Mexico City is a huge and polluted city where language difficulties take a back seat to the difficulty of breathing.

Disembarking the plane, I was hit full in the face by the furnace-like heat of the Mexican summer. I was supposed to have a ride to the language institute in Cuernavaca but my driver didn't show. After a few phone calls and inquiries—in Spanish, of course—I negotiated with an off-duty cab driver to drive me the two hours to Cuernavaca (he lived there) for the mere equivalent of 58 dollars! Tired and weary from the ordeal thus far, I arrived in Cuernavaca, hungry and still in need of a place to room since the language institute was closed for the day and nobody knew where I could find the proprietors. So, I rented a room for a fee of 26 dollars (cheap but my room and board were already paid for through the Institute) and started to count my blessings . . . I had just spent 85 dollars and several hours that day on an impromptu Spanish lesson!

The two weeks in Mexico sharpened my Spanish, but also showed me how little I really knew about the language and how far from fluency I really was.

Learning foreign languages in school is no substitute for living in a different country for an extended period of time. It is challenging having to think so much about things that require no effort at home. Going to the *mercado* (market) to shop, or to the local *lavanderia* (laundry), or the *boliche* (bowling alley), or to *el banco* (the bank), or any other public venue, inspired fear and loathing of the language and gave me a keen appreciation for fluency in *any* language.

While in Mexico studying I decided to write a daily journal, in Spanish. I commented on many things, including the weather, my Spanish lessons and social activities:

June 8, 1988:

Hace mucho calor hoy. No dormí bien anoche a causa del calor, estuve muy cansado todo el día. --- Las clases hoy fueron difíciles; estudiamos 'el pretérito' y 'los modismos.' --- Estoy aprendiendo mucho en mis clases y cada día estoy sentiendo mejor. --- Enrique vino a la casa desde las 8:00 hasta las 11:00. Él es muy buena onda. Hablamos por casi dos horas y bebimos unas cheves. Nos divertimos mucho. --- Despues, hice mi tarea hasta las 12:30 y despues, me fui a dormir.

By the end of two weeks in Mexico, I was mentally and emotionally drained from my efforts at perfecting Spanish. In the last entry in my journal I wrote, in Spanish:

I just realized tonight that there are no short cuts to learning a language. My vocabulary is expanding every day, my understanding and ability to form correct sentences gets better with each day also. But, for as much time and effort as I've put into it (and, counting college classes, I've put in a lot), the process is still painstakingly slow.

***

Besides scoring "brownie points" with my future wife (she lived in Spain for two years), all the study and learning of this language of my ancestors had little practical value in my life. None of my goals in life required, as a necessary condition, the ability to speak Spanish. Whether it was continuing my education or advancing in my job, knowledge of Spanish was inconsequential. If I lived in a Spanish-speaking country it would be a different matter, but I didn't. On the other hand, it is often the case that—regardless of ethnic or national origin—a good measure of English is necessary.

I recall visiting Europe in 1989 and talking with several young people from Sweden. We were sitting in the famous Hofbrau Haus in Munich drinking the thick, rich German beer and talking about the Wimbledon tennis championship that would be played the next day between Boris Becker and Sweden's Stephan Edberg. The Swedes, of course, were favoring Edberg (Becker won, however).

We were bleary-eyed from too much beer, laughing and talking and suddenly it struck me that, up until that moment, I didn't notice their fluency in English. In other words, they were so proficient that no attention was drawn to the language spoken, only to the content of what was said. These Swedes were speaking my native language so well that I was not even cognizant that they were non-native speakers. I mentioned this to one of them and his response resonated within me:

"Who else in the world speaks Swedish except Swedes? There is no incentive worldwide to speak Swedish, we have to speak English in order to survive as a nation."

By the time young people in Sweden finish High School, they have completed nearly 12 years of English! No wonder they are proficient articulators of our language.

English is the "second language" in many parts of the world because it is the *lingua franca* of international politics and business. Not to learn English puts those societies in a compromised position with respect to world development and economics.

Not so for us in the United States. We can go to almost any country in the world and find that people know how to speak English, well. We often learn foreign languages for personal amusement, for romantic notions, or because we plan to travel and think that by taking a class or two we will become proficient enough to speak with the natives. Sadly, it is often difficult to find places where people do not speak English better than we can speak their language. We would do well to follow their lead, which would only enhance our abilities to blend into their cultures as they have into ours and would help us to avoid the ethnocentricity that frequently plagues us Americans.

***

Communication problems are not only relegated to foreign language difficulties. At the age of two, I lost most of my hearing due to a severe bout of German Measles (Rubella). As a function of adaptation, I managed to communicate for many years by avoidance and by learning the myriad tricks of the hearing impaired.

Over the years I learned that I didn't need to hear in order to understand. The term "lip-reading" is misleading since most people communicate, serendipitously, with more than words; they use facial expressions, body language and vary the tone and loudness of their voice. I adapted to each situation by quickly picking up the context and looking for all the communication cues used by a speaker.

Up until about the 4th grade, I was able to hide my disability. However, at that time, the perennial "Hearing Bus" frequented my school and I was herded, along with my classmates, to the mandated hearing tests.

I flunked every hearing test that I ever took in school, though I found that this was a bonus for a grade school child. Since I flunked the tests, I was called out of class to retest. I thought it was cool and my classmates envied the fact that I was able to leave the doldrums of class and waltz out to the bus for a retest.

Further, I always passed the second test. This was because the well-meaning (but dense) technicians were an easy mark for a skilled tester like myself. The retest was a one-on-one affair that required me to raise my hand when I "heard a tone." I learned through practice that the technicians would tip their hand by inadvertently signaling me of the tone. I would wait for the invariable telltale sign: a wink of an eye, the raising of an eyebrow or some other unconscious quirk. I would raise my hand "on cue," so to speak and would buoyantly leave the bus, prideful and victorious as usual—earning safe passage until the next repeat of the assessment.

The bottom line of communication is this, if I want to communicate successfully, it is my responsibility. If I am discriminated against because of my hearing, or language it is because I have allowed it. I have a good measure of control over my grasp of a language and over the ways that others communicate with me. I have learned to adapt to the hearing world by changing the way that I "hear" and asking for others to be mindful of how they communicate.

I understand the dilemma of those who are disabled and yet realize that they must meet their challenges in positive ways that will allow them to achieve success—not only success that is limited to the realm of the disabled, but success that is unlimited and that will allow them to fulfill their dreams.

The hearing disabled, like those with language problems, must assimilate by distinguishing themselves in their efforts at communication with the general public. They must not accept mediocrity with respect to communication, but rather, should set high expectations for a success based on their needs within the society at large.

***

As a college teacher in the United States, it is vital that I possess a mastery of English. So too, my students need to learn English in order to succeed.

The conferral of a typical diploma (even one in a foreign language) carries the implicit assumption that the bearer has a more than casual knowledge of English and that by passing the classes leading to that degree, the student has been able to successfully parse the language of the conferring institution.

The best gift we can give our Spanish-speaking students is to help them perfect their

English, even in grade schools. While it may be a nice gesture to speak to children in their native language—and no doubt that would make them feel more comfortable—our most important obligation to our young students is to help them to speak, write, read and understand English and to move them along expeditiously in that direction.

At some point, every non-English-speaking parent must make a commitment to ensure that his or her child will ultimately master the dominant language. Parents must also continually encourage and cajole their children to pursue excellence and provide their children with every resource they need to succeed in developing language skills, which are also prerequisites for success in education.

Comfort is not the barometer of success and to delay the learning of English, even temporarily, will only serve to prolong the establishment of the public identity of our children, and delay the successes borne of acceptance and literacy.

There is nothing wrong with studying or understanding different languages—we should all celebrate this diversity—however, if people live and work in the United States, nothing should distract them from developing a command of the English language. Learning English should be the top priority and nothing should be allowed to impede or restrict our abilities and proficiencies because, ultimately, it is a command of the English language that will serve as our ticket to success. Whether in business, education, or life in general, English is the language of success in America. As a White Tortilla, I intuited this lesson at an early age, an age where language acquisition is still spontaneous and effectual.

Our educational institutions must help our students to excel in their world, a world that is rapidly changing and perpetually becoming more complex. They need to develop technological literacy as well as a command of traditional basic skills. As we deal with our students and children, we must explore and accept their differences and we must teach them to accept the differences of others. But we must not ignore, nor allow them to ignore, the language of success.

Chapter 5
The Church of my Youth

"[Man] regards God as an airman regards his parachute; it's there for emergencies but he hopes he'll never have to use it." ~ C. S. Lewis

It was Saturday and Herman "Pinche" Vasquez and I were on our way to catechism class at church in preparation for the Sacrament of Confirmation. Together, Confirmation, Baptism and the Eucharist constitute the sacraments of Christian initiation.

My mom was tired of forcing me to go to church and had decided that, after confirmation, I would be on my own. The way she looked at it, I had already received three of the sacraments: Baptism, Holy Eucharist, and Penance. The Sacrament of Matrimony would be up to me, and she didn't plan on being around for the Sacrament of Extreme Unction (Last Rites)—neither did I for that matter. So, she told me that I must be confirmed, but after that, she would not force me to go to church each week. That suited me fine—I had become disillusioned with the church years earlier and, at the tender age of 12, was at a low point in my faith.

"Hey Pinche, give me a hand here" I said. My friends and I had nicknamed Herman

"Pinche" (pronounced "peen-chee") because of his favorite utterance: "¡pinche cabrón!" Translated into English it means something that, if my mother had heard me utter the same words, would have cost *me* a mouthful of soap. Pinche uttered this expletive at least every couple of sentences, or so, and was well deserving of the moniker, I thought.

Pinche was small for his age (he didn't start growing up and filling out until late in high school), however he was absolutely fearless.

He gained a fearsome reputation in junior high school in an incident involving Junior Manoa, the biggest and meanest guy in school. Junior liked to intimidate everybody and, with his size, he could back it up. One day Junior took cuts in front of Pinche in the food line at the cafeteria and Pinche told him—in so many words—what he could do to his mother. A scuffle broke out that was quickly quelled by a teacher. That day after school, Junior caught up with Pinche on the way home from school and summarily beat the snot out of him.

For most people, that would have been the end of story, but the next day after school Pinche was waiting for Junior. With cuts and scrapes and a black eye showing, Pinche told Junior that he would be going home only over his dead body. Junior sneered and looked around at the sizable group of observers and promptly beat the crap out of Pinche again. In fact, he had to beat Pinche up for four days running because Pinche continued to pursue him and was determined to win, or die trying. Finally, the pressure grew too much for Junior.

Every day a larger crowd gathered and the tide of public opinion had shifted. Most of the kids started siding with Pinche and many even chided Junior for continuing to pick on someone who was completely overmatched. After that, Junior began to avoid Pinche like the plague. Pinche would seek him out both during and after school and Junior would hide out in bathrooms and take the long way home to avoid confrontation. From that day forward, nobody would mess with Pinche. He had earned the respect and the fear usually reserved for only the biggest and most ruthless. From that time forward, Pinche was "The Man."

As we stopped, Pinche put his two folded hands under my foot and lifted to boost me over the fence. Ironically, though we were headed toward God's most holy place on earth—the church—we were making a slight detour to commit a sin. The week before, while playing catch on our way to catechism, we had to retrieve our ball from over a fence and happened upon a field that had a berry bush with the biggest and ripest looking berries we had ever seen. We tasted them to be certain and, sure enough, those berries were to die for, which, as you will see, we nearly did. We decided that we would come back the next week and bring some giant freezer bags and help ourselves to some berries. So, as the plan went, we were going to climb over the fence into the yard, pack up the berries in our plastic bags and hide them somewhere until after catechism class, then we would pick them up on our way home.

After I was over the fence, Pinche climbed up and over. He was wiry and much stronger than me and he scaled that fence like he was some Special Forces commando, or something.

"¡*Ahh, pinche cabrón!*" he said as he stood shaking his hand and then pulling out a two-inch-long splinter.

"Hurry up Pinche, we're going to be late to church," I urged, knowing that Pinche was prone to becoming melodramatic over such things as splinters.

We proceeded to the bush and began picking berries. In no time we had our limits and proceeded to stash the berries in a hole in the side of a wooden shack where the boards had rotted out.

"There," I said. "Let's go! We'll come back and grab these when catechism lets out."

We reached the church in the nick of time, rushing past Father Grácias, who was simultaneously looking at his watch and glowering at us over his bifocals.

The Catholic Church is rich in tradition: liturgical ceremonies and the accompanying symbolism illustrate lessons of church doctrine. According to Catholic beliefs, God is all-powerful (omnipotent) and all-knowing (omniscient), which includes knowing not only everything that *has* happened, but everything that *will* happen (prescient). He knows what you have done, both good and bad (like Santa, only infinitely better), and he knows even your thoughts. (Thus the import of Jimmy Carter's famous admission that he'd "lusted after women in his heart many times.") In short, you can't pull anything over on God.

The architecture of any given church is designed to teach you something about the nature and character of God. The typically high ceilings and archways depict the majesty of God and graphically illustrate the vast chasm between an imperfect man and a perfectly good and just God. The tabernacle and other church articles as well as the vestments worn by the priests, are made of gold and precious stones and fine materials symbolizing the perfect nature of God.

Later, while visiting Europe as an adult, I was awestruck by the magnificence of the churches there. The church in Santiago de Compostela (Spain) was an exceptional example of the miracle of Gothic architecture and a relic of faith. The church of "Santiago" was named after the apostle James, one of the "inner-circle" of Jesus' disciples: Peter, James and John. This huge and ornate cathedral is purported to have the earthly remains of the apostle James. Millions of Christians make pilgrimages to worship the vestige of James at this church, though it has always seemed incredible to me that people are so quick to worship the creature, than the Creator.

But by far the most awe-inspiring aspect of my own church, from my 12-year-old vantage point, was the cast figure of Christ hanging on the cross. The agonies attendant to having the nails hammered into his hands and feet, the crown of thorns pushed onto his head and the heavy gash in his side, through which poured "blood and water," were the perfect demonstration of his sacrifice and love for mankind, according to the Bible. No matter where you sat in the church, his sad eyes would be looking right at you, penetrating your soul with the thought that somehow you personally were responsible for his suffering and death.

The Catholic church of my youth was filled with mystery. The miraculous changing of the bread and the wine into the body and blood of Christ is an awesome testament to the personal epiphany of God to his faithful (believe me this is no small thing when you are gagging on the host and can't dislodge it with anything as profane as your finger). The recital of the mass in Latin, and the instantaneous forgiveness of sin via confession, repentance and penance served to remind the faithful that God is holy and is alone worthy of our praise.

The miracle of forgiveness happened to be perfectly timed with the sin that Pinche and I had just committed. We were about an hour away from confession, after which we would be off scot-free, according to our warped understanding of Catholic creed.

Regardless of the object lessons of the faith, I was not destined to stay in the Catholic Church (a fact that God already knew of course). The problem stemmed from my bad experiences in Catholic school combined with the impersonal nature of the mass—I mean if you didn't know Latin, it was a snoozer—and the fearful image of God as portrayed through the teachings of the sisters and priests. The doctrine of a vengeful God—reinforced by vengeful nuns—did little to attract me to the religion and was just too much for an insecure boy like myself to handle.

Interestingly, years later after I became a "heathen" by embracing a different religion, I was delighted to attend a Catholic service with my mother and noted that the church had a different focus—services were more "people friendly." Masses were conducted in the common language of the people, there was guitar playing and singing of folk hymns, people were encouraged to read and study the Bible, which was translated into the English language.

This made my mother, and probably most traditionalists, a bit queasy. Instead of chanting impersonal and often unintelligible phrases, the faithful were accountable in ways never imagined before.

Reciting doctrines in English, such as the Apostolic or Nicene Creeds, now made one accountable to follow through on the maxims being espoused. Hearing scripture in English—not to mention a more user-friendly translation—gave the average person real insight into the will of God, regardless of the expository teachings of the priest.

These were all good changes, in my estimation, but they came too late in my spiritual journey to have any effect. As a youngster contemplating confirmation, I was weary of what I considered a legalistic and ultratraditional church. I wanted more freedom, less ritual and less fear. Perhaps I was just traversing the rebelliousness of youth. Or, perhaps the hormones of puberty created an inherent conflict between religion and my own hedonic tendencies.

Whatever the case, after leaving the Catholic Church I became more intent on relationship than religion and some years later I penned the following verse:

There is no joy without God.
No life save in his name.
Wisdom and human knowledge pulsate,
fade and come to naught as we struggle to
reason his existence.
The filling comes and then goes,
I know not when nor sometimes why.
Yet, each glimmer and spark of spirit that
flies, though left unattended,
yields more fruit than countless hours
of striving for what only seems to be.
To know, to truly know, is the greatest
treasure one can hope for.
In this life we know in part, but then, fully.
And yet, I know him and without doubt.
He has made it known, that I might reflect
and be sure. Test and be quiet.
For in him and through him all things exist
and come to be.
Indeed, he formed them yesterday,
as today.

After confession, Pinche and I left the church with clean hearts and ready to collect our stash of berries. Upon arriving at the stash hole, we found to our surprise that the bags of berries had been shredded open. They were a mess and we couldn't figure out why until we looked out toward the berry bush. There we saw the culprits, the property owner and his very large German shepherd that had apparently sniffed out our plunder and broke into the contents.

We didn't have long to consider the consequences because that dog saw us and started toward us at a gallop and with bad intent, I surmised. With hackles bristled and fangs foaming that dog was gaining on us. We were running as fast as we could toward the fence and safety. It was then that I came to a fateful conclusion: we were not going to make it. We were running out of room and the dog was gaining too fast. In the heat of the moment, I hit Pinche with an elbow and he went down. I scaled that fence like I was a Special Forces commando, the last thing I felt was dog spit running down my collar and the last thing I heard was, "¡*Pinche cabro-oooooooohhhhn!*"

Fortunately, Pinche lived to tell the story and we had something else to confess the next week. We completed our spiritual transition by perfecting our faith through the Sacrament of Confirmation, following which neither of us attended church for the ensuing few years.

The religion of my youth shaped my sense of right and wrong, good and bad, important and unimportant. Apostasy from the church notwithstanding, I had a strong set of values that were shaped by the dogma of Catholicism. My parents too were deeply affected by their religion—their morals guiding them towards their philosophies of life. This seems an especially important point given that the lessons of the White Tortilla are riddled with elements of Christian charity, respect and forgiveness.

Confirmation marked a time of transformation. I was spiritually bankrupt for the next six years—a White Tortilla adrift of the religion of his youth. Tragically, Pinche—who became a real Special Forces commando nine years later—ended up in a nondescript grave somewhere on the wrong side of the Cambodian border.

Henrietta "Ricky" Merrill, age 13

Norberto "Bert" Diaz, age 20

Bert Diaz at Franco's Market, age 17

Diaz Market, circa 1963

Ricky and Bert, circa 1943

David and Bert

David in Catholic School Uniform

High School Graduation 1971

Bert enjoying his favorite pastime: fishing.

Ricky at age 88 years.

Chapter 6
La Comida Mexicana

"If you reject the food, ignore the customs, fear the religion and avoid the people, you might better stay home." ~ James Michener

Visiting my grandmother's house when I was young was typically a painful affair. For one thing, I didn't speak Spanish and everything my grandmother said had to be painstakingly translated for me. I suffered the double embarrassment of not being able to communicate and being cooed over by my grandmother and aunts—something a shy boy hates. Further, we didn't go there very often since there were some residual animosities between my parents and my grandmother.

During our monthly visits, what made the biggest impression on me were the smells. Upon entering the house, I was immediately taken aback by the odors of weathered furniture, dusty linens and rotting window shades. This disturbed me usually because it gave off the aura of decay, aging and death. It made me uncomfortable and I erroneously associated this feeling with the Mexican culture.

However, after I would habituate myself to those smells, there came the sweet and pungent aromas of food. First, I would notice the herbs that were used by my grandmother for so many things. She grew her own herbs—from medicinal herbs to cooking herbs—thyme, rosemary, oregano, cilantro, basil, cumin and so many more. These would lie fresh or in dried bunches on the countertop, waiting not only to be used for medicines, but in soups, stews and the panoply of delicious meals cooked in that home.

My grandmother was a physician of sorts and had learned her craft from her mother and grandmother. They shared, and she memorized, hundreds of recipes for herbal concoctions that would heal most ailments.

I had been on the receiving end of a variety of her folk-medicine remedies. She would slice potatoes and place them on my forehead when I had a fever or headache, supposedly to leach out the bad humors (i.e., reduce fevers), or have me sip various teas and soups as indicated for colds, coughs and other ailments. I would have balms rubbed on my chest for phlegm, and hot herbal compresses for sinus problems.

La comida Mexicana, the Mexican meal, is full of wondrous specialties. My favorites include *Albondigas* (meatball) soup, *Sopa de tortilla* (tortilla soup), *Nopales* (a pork stew cooked with cactus), *Chiles Rellenos* (stuffed peppers), *Menudo* (tripe soup), and *Chorizo* (you don't want to know).

The paradox between the smells of aging and decay—the initial smells of the household—and the smells of food that conspired to create contentment and a sense of *familia,* was difficult to resolve. The smells of the Mexican table were overwhelming and wonderful and gave me a feeling of contentment and calm.

Anaheim chiles were roasted over an open fire, waiting to be stuffed with cheese and fried in a fluffy egg batter. Fragrant and green, fresh chopped cilantro was spread over salsa, soups and *camarón* (shrimp).

I heard the constant grinding of cornmeal and the patter of hands as my aunts hand-rolled and patted out perfectly round, fresh tortillas and then cooked them on a *comal* (flat griddle)—the inviting smell wafting throughout the house.

As we would sit down to eat, all barriers melted into nothingness. Filling our faces with warm, rich food, we found other ways to bridge our differences: a wink of an eye, a finger point to request a pass of the dish, a smile, or even the inadvertent smacking of lips or belch, all worked together to build community and communicate love.

In the Mexican tradition of that household, food and family became part of the same verb: "to feed" and "to family" became one inseparable element of the condition of being Mexican.

My mother was no slouch when it came to crafting an ethnic repast. One of my fondest and most comforting memories of childhood was waking every morning to the smells of breakfast. Permeating the house on their way to my bedroom were the smells of eggs and bacon, chorizo, potato pancakes and sausage.

My mother always had a pot of beans boiling. Beans—the Mexican staple. Pinto beans are an indispensable component of burritos, nachos and taquitos, and the perfect companion to rice and salsa.

Cooking beans is an art. First, my mother would soak them overnight—"to leach out the *pedos* [farts]," my dad used to say. Then she would boil them adding salt, pepper, onions and her secret ingredient: a slab of bacon. We would eat beans as a soup the first day or two because the broth made by the boiled beans was so delicious. Then, my mother would refry the beans in bacon fat and we would eat them with breakfast, lunch or dinner. ¡*Qué ricos*!

Spanish rice, another staple, was browned lightly in oil and mixed with water, tomato sauce and onions, and then spiced with *comino* (cumin) and bay leaves. When cooked in a medium pan for about 20 minutes, the product is light and fluffy, golden brown and succulent.

Beans and rice are the ideal accoutrement of almost any meal. These two staples represent the generosity and vigor of *la comida Mexicana* and are the canvas that supports the *muralista* of the kitchen.

Besides her specialties, my mom was creative in the kitchen and could cook a meal using almost any ingredient. I bet she could cook for a week—with only canned Spam as her main ingredient—and never make the same meal twice. And it would be *good.*

***

Integrating the experience of *la comida Mexicana* into the American lifestyle is a very tricky business. I remember the anticipation of my first sleep over. I was about 8 years old and I was going to stay at a friend's house. Jimmy Deese lived with his parents on the local Navy "Seabee" base. In preparation for my visit, my mother used the opportunity to culturally sensitize me.

"David, I want you to be careful how you act over at your friend's house," my mother's voice and demeanor suddenly a picture of concern. "You can't eat with tortillas there like you do at home."

I thought she was referring to my habit of using only tortillas as my utensils for eating. I learned this from my father and he from his father, and so on. Not much of a trick really, you simply break off a bit of tortilla, then tear it in two again and you have two little scoops that together can be used to direct food into your mouth—an edible replacement apparatus for spoons and forks, so to speak.

"I know, I know, I'll be careful." What I thought she meant was that I should use a fork along with my tortilla, but she clarified.

"No David, I mean that your friends parents may not even have tortillas to eat. They may use bread instead."

No problem there, I had used bread before, but it is much less efficient when it comes to using as an eating utensil.

What I would later learn was that what was considered acceptable conduct at *la comida Mexicana*, may not be acceptable in other settings. I learned that, in order to assimilate into the public at large, I must regulate and control my culturally defined behavior.

My mother would also explain that not everyone from other cultures would appreciate some of my favorite foods. As unbelievable as it seemed to my young mind, there were people out there who would not enjoy eating beef tripe, cactus and cow tongue. Imagine that!

Thus, some of my most prized possessions, the delicacies of the Mexican table, might make me unacceptable to others and would have to be put aside. Along with obtaining a good education and being able to master the English language, adapting to the cultural traits of the majority, and the acceptance entailed therein, became the third "person" of the holy trinity of assimilation.

It became evident to me that my parents often adjusted their own tastes to accommodate others. When we would have certain dinner guests, for instance, my mother would make "americanized," generic Mexican meals. Tacos, beans and rice—no tortillas, we ate with forks—or, enchiladas and salad. But none of the really wonderful, ripe, pungent flavors of *la comida Mexicana*, and very little of the spice: mild, insipid salsa, instead of that spiked with Jalapeno or Serrano peppers.

The notion of setting aside one's own cultural practices in deference to others may seem odd to the reader; however, it is a common practice. I was never so convinced of this than after my first trip to Italy.

In the mid 1980s, I was selected along with four other business professionals, to represent the United States to Central Italy in a program sponsored by Rotary International. The purpose of the Group Study Exchange (GSE) was to send young professionals to tour a host country (this program is active in over 100 countries) and learn as much as possible, while accurately communicating important information about our country to the hosts. We were, in effect, "ambassadors" of peace and goodwill.

In the spring of 1986, the GSE took us to sixteen cities in seven weeks. Most of these cities were in central Italy and on the Adriatic coast. The selection process for this program was rigorous, as it was very important that our individual group members could accept cultural differences and adapt to the Italian culture including the language and customs.

Our first two weeks of the program started in Los Angeles at the Berlitz Language School for language and "cultural sensitivity" training. During our training we were taught to observe many of the practices of the host country, especially the local eating habits, so as not to offend our hosts and to better assimilate into their culture.

One piece of advice for dealing with the inevitable was given us by our teacher: "When in doubt, watch and see what everyone else does and do the same." Good advice, as it turned out.

During the first week in Rome, we enjoyed a feast at the home of one prominent Rotarian. The meal was progressing wonderfully until they served a large bowl of sea shrimp, whole, with heads and shells attached. We all froze, wondering what to do next. None of us had encountered such a culinary crisis in our limited experience. We were at a loss for action. Our host Enrico, comprehending the situation, took one of the shrimps, ceremoniously broke off the head and proceeded to suck the brains out. We all looked at each other, and with just a hint of a smile, followed suit. The rest of the process of pulling off the legs and shells, our hands dripping with shrimp juice and olive oil, was an enjoyable bonding experience and provided me with a lasting image of cultural diversity. Literally then, when in Rome, do as the Romans!

This type of experience has taught me to see the practices of my parents in a different light. Though we all have a right to exercise our cultural traditions, we should not exercise those rights indiscriminately or at the expense of the cultural practices of others. Certainly a spirit of compromise, respect and deference should come into play as we commingle in a diverse environment.

My parents were the outsiders trying to fit in, trying not to offend the hosts (or guests), trying to assimilate. When they altered their meals or their behavior, or their language, it was to show respect for their hosts and distinguish themselves in this regard—to be, as the apostle Paul noted, "all things to all men."

Chapter 7
Give Until it Hurts

"I have found that among its other benefits, giving liberates the soul of the giver." ~ Maya Angelou

Fourth grade was a breath of fresh air for me. My mother had pardoned me from Catholic school, with credit for time served, I guess. I was now in public school and was enjoying my newfound freedoms.

Public school just seemed to be more fun. We had all kinds of after-school activities, sports and special events. During my first year, we had the opportunity to build and race rockets at the "Saturday Rocket Races."

These rockets had to be constructed according to certain specifications; they were made from wood with a rubber band inside the rocket that was attached to a propeller. Two pieces of heavy-gauge wire protruded from the topside of the rocket so it could be hung from the tracking wire. To race it, you simply wound up the propeller, set the rocket on the wire and then let go. The rocket went zooming away down the wire and towards the finish line.

As usual, my father helped me build my project. I had painted my rocket "Candy-Apple

Red" with flame decals and my favorite number "5" on each side. On the morning of the event, my dad and I conducted last-minute tests. Our family market was open on Saturday and dad was working but he took the time to help me test my rocket by removing the signs he had draped over wires above the meat counter, allowing me to slide my rocket on the wires.

"Remember to wind the propeller clockwise," said my dad as he wound it up and set it on the wire. When he let go of the propeller, that rocket flew across the wire like a "BB" spit out of my "Daisy" BB-Gun. I was so happy and excited about taking my rocket to the race, that I didn't even practice winding it up myself.

At the schoolyard, there were a hundred kids or more, some with their parents and some without. They were standing in line two-by-two, waiting to approach the official race wires and the single elimination contest.

After waiting in line for 20 minutes or so, it was my turn to race. I was matched up against Casey Bemis, who sported a solid black rocket with skull and crossbones adorning the sides. As I started to wind up the propeller, I became confused and couldn't remember which way to wind it. In my haste and anxiety, I settled on counterclockwise.

The starter said, "Ready. Set. Go!" and I let go of the propeller. As the propeller spun furiously, my rocket surged forward about 4 inches and then backward about 6 inches and then just froze in one place until it was all spun out.

Some of the kids laughed and one of the referees patted me on the back and said, "Tough luck kid."

I walked back to our store with my head down and tears in my eyes. When I got to the store, I trudged back to the meats section and sat in the corner.

My dad was just coming out of the meat cooler when he saw me. "What happened *mi'jo*? How did it go?"

I told him the painful story and started to cry. He stroked my head and started to take off his butcher smock. "Let's go David," he said.

As we walked by the front counter, he told my mom that we would be back in a half hour or so. We drove back to the schoolyard in my dad's old Chevy neither of us saying a word.

When we arrived at the schoolyard, my dad talked to the referee and, before I knew it, I was back at the start line. This time, dad coached me as I wound up the propeller and let that rocket fly. I didn't win the race, but my pride and confidence soared as I watched my creation sail toward the finish line straight and true.

This story typifies my dad. He was a giver: he gave his time, energy, expertise and money to help others achieve; and not just his children or his friends, but anyone within his sphere of influence that had a need. This trait had nothing to do with his ethnic origin or race, but it *was* consistent with his philosophy of assimilation. To assimilate successfully, he believed that we must distinguish ourselves among our peers. But how can that be achieved, he wondered, if a person does not have the wherewithal to achieve their goals? That's where my dad saw his purpose. Whenever he would see a person facing some obstacle to the achievement of a dream or goal, he would step in and do whatever he could to help.

I never fully appreciated this until after my father died. At his funeral there were many people—some I knew, many I didn't—but they came one at a time to tell me their story of how my dad had helped them.

One person was learning the butcher trade and my dad took time to come over and help teach him the finer points, even giving him his first set of knives. Another person happened to mention to my dad that he was dropping out of school because he needed money—my dad gave him money for registration and then loaned him more money to get him through the year.

There was one family who lived across the street from our market—a single mother and her two teenage daughters. The three of them used to come into the store from time to time and steal groceries. The mother or one of the daughters would keep whoever was at the checkout stand busy, while the other two would pocket merchandise. After giving the situation some thought, my father took two large bags of groceries over to their house and said he knew they were having a difficult time and would they accept a contribution of groceries once a month until they could better afford them. In time, they not only stopped stealing, but they also paid off their line of credit and would regularly bring over baked cookies, cakes and other goodies to share with us.

These stories, and many more, astounded me and I began to realize that my father wasn't just generous to my family, but to everyone he came in contact with.

One thing I do remember was that I had to be careful what I wished for around my dad. He took all wishes literally and wanted to make them happen. It embarrassed me if I was always on the receiving end of his generosity. Further, it made me want to emulate his behavior, to give back to him in ways that I could: mowing the lawns, sweeping, pulling weeds, or whatever.

There were three characteristics about my father's giving that I thought were especially noteworthy: First, he would give with no expectation of anything in return (truly selfless giving is accomplished without expectations or coercion). He never really wanted people to repay him; he was content that he was able to help out. Second, he would give quietly and without fanfare (a silent gift)—most of the stories of his giving I learned about much later from my mother and others who had benefited. And third, he would give until it hurt—which was why he was always out of time and money. My mother would have to give him an allowance—out of his own paycheck—because whatever he had, he would give to others. He really gave until it hurt.

There is a biblical story that comes to mind that seems an appropriate illustration: the parable of the "widow's mite."

And [Jesus] sat down opposite the treasury, and began observing how the multitude were putting money into the treasury; and many rich people were putting in large sums. And a poor widow came and put in two small copper coins, which amount to a cent. And calling His disciples to Him, He said to them, 'Truly I say to you, this poor widow put in more than all the contributors to the treasury; for they all put in out of their surplus, but she, out of her poverty, put in all she owned, all she had to live on. (The Gospel of Mark, 12:41-44)

The widow didn't give out of her surplus, but instead out of her basic necessities for living. She gave until it hurt.

I have tried to emulate the philosophy of "giving till it hurts" and have taught my children, and even my students, to do the same.

There is an assignment that I allow my students to complete near the end of each semester called the "Silent Gift" assignment.[6] The concept of the silent gift is simple: the giver must give a special gift to someone, once a day for 5 days. The gifts are open to creativity: kind and encouraging notes, flowers, a batch of cookies, household chores, etc. The recipient of the gifts can be almost anyone; however, no one, especially the recipient, can know the source of the gifts.

I emphasize to my students that truly selfless giving, the kind that expresses genuine care, should be accomplished without the expectation of reciprocation. In other words, they are to give anonymously so there is no expectation of something in return. Many students opt to complete the silent gift assignment and I have heard reports from these students that amply describe the value of this type of giving. In short, there is plenty of emotional and spiritual capital to be gained as a result of selfless giving. Giving enhances our health and happiness and truly liberates the soul of the giver.

Many in the ranks of the rich and famous give to charitable organizations and causes. I don't claim to know their motives, but I am suspicious. All the fanfare and news press associated with the giving lends a circus atmosphere and seems to be something conjured up by the publicity agents. Further, the tax relief provided by the "donation" may serve as a superseding motive.

As we look back and assess our lives periodically, or as the end draws near, there is value in knowing that we have accomplished something of significance in our life, that we have contributed to the world in some positive way.

Giving is one of the measures of a successful life. It doesn't have to be money and it doesn't have to be much. People who continually look for opportunities to give, and who give without expectations of reciprocation, without drawing attention to their giving, and who give to the extent that it stretches their resources, will reap true rewards and a lasting confidence that they have made a real difference in their world.

This indeed is a lesson of the White Tortilla. Giving distinguishes us in life and helps us make a positive contribution to those within our sphere of influence, including ourselves.

Chapter 8
Ethnocentric Differences

"The greatest problem in communication is the illusion that it has been accomplished."
~ George Bernard Shaw

Louie "Gazpacho" Lopez was sitting by the side of the road hurling his guts onto the litter-strewn asphalt. He drank too much Tequila on the way to a high school football game. Again. He had a habit of chugging booze until he regurgitated; a weekly ritual of bingeing and purging the soul, I guess. So, we waited as he puked, hoping that our Port Hueneme High 'Vikings' would fare well in the game without our immediate presence.

Louie played on the high school basketball team along with Franco "Pizza Face" DeBernardinis and me. The three of us had been driving to Camarillo High School to watch our football team compete when Gazpacho got the "urge."

"Hey Gazpacho, save me the big pieces," I chided, adding insult to injury.

"Get losssst Diazzzz!" Gazpacho slurred as spit and puke oozed from his mouth. "I hate your guts," he continued under his breath.

We called Louie "Gazpacho," not after the soup (though there were certain similarities in the products), but because of the unique sound he made as he puked. He tended to expel consonants in a forceful and wheezing pattern that sounded (if not looked) like the popular cold soup.

Louie groaned as he started to heave again, "Gzzz-sp-choohhh, gzzz-sp-choohhh," he gargled. "Ohhhhh man," he moaned. "Just leave me here, I'm gonna die."

"Hey Franco, give me a hand here," I said as I started to pull Gazpacho up and toward the backseat of Franco's car. "We're never gonna make the game if we don't hurry."

"Listen to me Gazpacho, eh?" said Franco in his thick Italian accent. "Don'a you puke in *la machina*, okay? *Va bene! Andiamo,* let's go, David."

We made it to the football game late and left Gazpacho passed out in the backseat. All he remembered of the game was staring through the back window at the stadium lights—which were spinning and dancing like so many fireflies—and fighting down the relentlessly surging bile in his throat.

***

One of the things I remember about high school was the common penchant for assigning nicknames to one another. It seemed like none of those we hung out with were immune from having their name appended with some derogatory jibe.

Franco was referred to as "Pizza Face," not only because he was Italian, but also because he had what looked like a terminal case of pimples. I had a nickname too, but I'm not telling what it was. The point is that high-school-aged young people are notoriously insecure and putting-down others around them helps them to deal with their insecurities, albeit in a non-productive manner.

The nicknames were most often derogatory in nature and, in many cases, were not used consistently. They were often doled out, as needed, to serve as delimiters of status distinctions within our group. In other words, nicknames were freely dispensed when any of us decided that someone needed to be put in his place, or reminded of his fallibility. Of course, this was merely a form of discrimination, which often reinforced cultural stereotypes.

However, discrimination was not always related to ethnicity. Young and immature people like us were equal opportunity discriminators. We simply looked for anything different: fat, skinny, tall, short, wearing clothes that were not "in," or any other form of "looking funny." Casey Bemis was called "Butterball" because he was fat, and Stevie Lupus was "Gandhi" because he was skinny.

The key to understanding discrimination, I think, is to realize that it is about *differences*—of *any* kind. Not just ethnic differences but anything that can be used as leverage by the discriminator to artificially elevate his or her status in contrast to others.

The challenges of many adult relationships have their origin in the discriminatory patterns of our youth. As people grow up and move away from home, they encounter more complex relationships with others with whom they have less in common. Many of the difficulties in relationships between husband and wife, boyfriend and girlfriend, teammates, roommates and other friends, are a result of what I like to call "ethnocentric differences." Ethnocentric differences are those that result from the way we have been raised and engender the common notion that the way *we* believe or do things is the *right* way.

Each of us comes from a different background. Economic, social and geographical differences, as well as those of religion, language, customs and family size, all conspire to create very different sets of values and life practices. When you have two or more people in a relationship, the typical problems that result are often attributable to the different lifestyle practices and values inherited from their familial and cultural backgrounds. Not all ethnocentric differences relate specifically to ethnicity; however, it is often difficult to separate ethnicity and culture from the other aspects of our lives.

***

The football game was turning into a blowout in favor of Camarillo High—we didn't win many games that year. Franco and I had smuggled some beers into the game and sipped them through straws in diversionary soda cups. We quickly grew bored with the game and decided to leave early.

Back at the car we checked on Gazpacho who was still passed out—but also still breathing—fortunately. So, we hopped into the car and drove off in search of food. We always became hungry when we were drinking and usually stopped at Denny's or McDonald's. Both establishments were located on the main "cruise" street—Saviers Road—in downtown Oxnard.

All the guys I hung with committed their extra time, money and affection to their cars. We would spend many weekends immersed in mechanical nirvana. Six or eight of us would pull up on someone's front lawn, or under the shade of a tree, and pop our hoods till the impending sunset announced "cruising time." We worked diligently with hoods up and heads down in the engine compartments—tweaking and cranking and scraping knuckles. Whatever cars would start after all the tinkering would be commandeered for the evening cruise. Any weekend night we could find our friends cruising up and down Saviers in the cars they so meticulously maintained.

Franco's Chevy Camaro had a high-performance 327 engine and a distinctive neon-orange paint job. It was jacked up in the rear with traction bars and had the high-pitched rumble of exhaust headers.

No low-riders for us—leave the asphalt-scraping, furry dashboards and chain-link steering wheels to the "Colonia" gangs. Nothing more than electro-pneumatic Pogo-Sticks, in our opinion.

We were running low on cash, having spent most of our weekly rations on beer and, in Gazpacho's case, Tequila. We were scrounging up our last bit of cash to buy some food and gas for the car (we were running on fumes). Fortunately, gas at that time was 25 cents per gallon. (Yes, really.) So, with a buck-fifty in change, we put a couple gallons in the Camaro and still had enough for a Big Mac each and large fries.

We sat in the McDonald's parking lot and watched as other cruisers drove up and down Saviers, through the McDonald's parking lot and then around again for yet another cruise. Cruising was cool. It was a way for us guys to show off—our cars, our "girlfriends," our coolness—or perhaps just our conceit.

There was Jake Jensen with his yellow and black striped "Super Bee" and Charlie Mendoza in a Ford "Boss" 429. As we passed each other on the road or in the parking lot, we would tip our heads up and back, signifying, "What's up?" Quite the sight—all those rocking heads borne along by souped-up, multi-colored, air-polluting gas-hogs.

I looked in the back seat of Franco's car to conduct a postmortem on Gazpacho. He was oblivious to the world—still passed out and didn't even have any cash (we checked his pockets). Occasionally snorting and with drool streaming from the side of his mouth, he was only temporarily avoiding what would be a merciless hangover.

I guess we couldn't be too hard on Gazpacho since we would each take our turns getting "hammered" from week-to-week.

When I think about it, I find it interesting that Americans have such a maladaptive method of drinking alcohol. Maybe it's because most of us learned how to drink from imitating our friends and acquaintances.

I learned to drink in high school. Not in gym class or history, but on Friday nights before football games and dances—"coached" by my friends. The basic knack, as I interpreted it, was to ingest copious amounts of alcohol in a short period of time. My buddies and I usually accomplished this feat by taking cans of beer, turning them upside down and putting a hole in the bottom of the can. Then, covering the hole with a finger, we would pop the tab on the top of the can, tip the can to our lips and uncover the hole. This allowed us to chug the entire contents of the can in 5 or 6 seconds. The recipe for "success" then, was to "supercharge" three or four 16-oz cans in this manner until we were sufficiently stuporous or comatose (read: dumb and dumber). Other acceptable means of achieving these states were drinking games like "Quarters," "Caps," or any other similar and reliable methods.

These idiosyncratic practices are peculiarly American in that very few other countries practice alcohol abuse to the extent and with the same fervor that we do in the United States. Even countries that are known for their drinking habits have a more rational approach when it comes to teaching their young people to drink.

While visiting Italy in 1986, I became interested in the drinking habits of the young people in the country. I found, to my surprise, a relative lack of interest in alcohol as a social drink. And yet, children are introduced to alcohol when they are quite young. It is common to see parents mixing wine with water to give to young children during meal times. Alcohol is almost always prevalent at the Italian meal and, thus, identified as a food rather than a social beverage.

Nightclubs in Italy are popular with young adults. There is usually a cover charge of "two drinks" levied by the establishment. As I traveled from city to city and attended these clubs with young Italians, usually between the ages of 20-30, I never once saw anyone purchase alcohol drinks. Soda and mineral water were always the choices. There seemed to be a general disinterest in alcohol as a "party" drink. The "happy hour" phenomenon is a predominantly American concept.

As with other ethnocentric practices, alcohol consumption is influenced by cultural mores. In my opinion, families should promote responsible drinking by linking alcohol consumption to meals and by providing their adolescent children the opportunities to drink safely and healthfully. Young people should learn their drinking habits from their parents, in a loving and safe environment, not from their peers.

Regardless, it is inevitable that many young people will experience problems with alcohol. Problems caused by alcohol require attention and careful, caring communication. We need to communicate the potential dangers of alcohol early to our young people and teach them safe, sane, and moderate consumption techniques.

We can learn lessons from European countries and other cultures that expose their children to alcohol at an early age and demystify the beverage. They teach a respect for the power of the beverage while integrating it into the daily meals. Mealtime consumption allows dialog and supervision and provides opportunities to teach lessons of common sense and health.

***

When I was in college, I roomed with a friend that I had known for 18 years. We attended almost every grade together from kindergarten through high school. I couldn't have asked for a better roommate, we were best friends. However, living together created some unique situations that tested our friendship.

In most situations, we were perfectly matched: we liked the same foods (e.g., Hamburger Helper and Macaroni and Cheese), music (70's rock) and beer (Coors, but none of that "light" garbage).

When it came to household chores we had a well-oiled working relationship. For example, we would usually wait until there were no dishes left in the cupboards or utensils in the drawers—because they were all out on the sink dirty—before we would wash dishes. Then, we would take turns performing this task.

I remember one day, it was his turn to wash dishes. He started the water running and put a good dose of soap in the dishwater and then walked down the hall for a minute to ask something of our neighbor. While he was gone I thought I would be a good roommate and start washing some of the dishes for him. I reached into the soapy dishwater and what do you think I pulled out? A knife. A *sharp* knife. In the soapy dishwater. I was puzzled. What kind of fool puts a sharp knife into the soapy dishwater? Maybe it was a mistake, an accident. I checked the water again. Sure enough, no mistake. I pulled out *another* sharp knife. Out of the *soapy dishwater*. This guy was an *idiot*! Everybody *knows* that you don't put sharp knives in soapy dishwater because somebody like me could reach in and cut himself! I cursed him and his upbringing, wondering how he had lived this long without lacerating himself to death. I was seething when he came back into the kitchen.

"What the hell do you think you're doing?" I screamed as he fell back a couple of steps. "Don't you *know* that you never put sharp knives in soapy dishwater where someone could cut their hand off? What were you *thinking*?"

I'll never forget the simplicity of his response: "Well, that's the way we always did it at our house."

It was apparent that family members at his house didn't thrust their hands into soapy dishwater because they knew there were sharp knives lurking there. While, at my house, we could thrust away because we knew the sharp knives were safely sitting on the counter top.

My mistake, which was common enough, was to consider the situation as an ethical dilemma (something that is right or wrong) instead of an ethnocentric dilemma (something that works or doesn't work and is related to how we were raised). This situation had nothing to do with "right and wrong." It was a matter of two people, raised in widely different backgrounds, who must now decide how they will compromise to make things *work* in their *current* living environment.

In conversations with students, I have heard many examples of how ethnocentric differences create problems in relationships.

One young woman related the story of the "growing chair." I asked her what she meant by this and she explained. "Well, when I take off my dirty clothes, I put them in a dirty clothes hamper in my closet. But my roommate puts her dirty clothes on the back of her chair. As the week goes by, her chair continually 'grows'—piled higher and higher with her dirty, stinking laundry."

"So," I prompted, "what was she *supposed* to do?"

"Well, everybody *knows* that, when you take off your dirty clothes, you are *supposed* to put them away in some type of container in the closet. I can't believe what a *slob* my roommate is!"

This young woman was essentially saying that there is a right way and a wrong way to archive, as it were, dirty clothes. And, *of course*, her way was the right way.

As it turned out, her roommate grew up as an only child and her room was her domain. She could do as she pleased as long as no one else was affected. As long as the door remained closed, she was free to nourish her growing chair. However, the first young woman shared a room with two other sisters. They had determined from the beginning that, to keep peace in the house, they would need to clean up their own mess—including storing dirty laundry in a personal hamper in the closet.

As we grow older and start developing personal relationships with those outside our family and close acquaintances—that is, those from radically different backgrounds—we start seeing our own behavior, not just as *one* way, but as the *right* way.

The answer to the dilemma of these two roommates was that they would have to sit down and communicate with each other about the perceived problem and then brainstorm how to modify their practices in ways that would work for both of them.

I would be willing to bet that the causes of almost all problems in relationships can be reduced to ethnocentric differences. Solving these problems requires sustained, careful and caring communication. If we value our relationships, then we owe it to ourselves to work to sustain and improve those relationships. We must also see that our differences have nothing to do with right and wrong, but instead they are the products of our upbringing and the myriad factors that are related to our cultural, economic, and geographic backgrounds.

The first step in caring communication is to actually do it. Don't put it off.

Many of us want to avoid the confrontations that are typically associated with communication. Avoiding communication is like trying to prevent a pot of water from boiling over by placing a brick on the lid. As the pressure builds, the lid will continue to lift. As we continue to avoid communication, we are effectively putting more bricks on the lid. No matter how many bricks we pile on, the lid will eventually blow—and the damage will be great.

The day I found that sharp knife in the soapy dishwater was the day I had reached my boiling point. It wasn't that the knife issue was such a terrible problem in itself—it was just one more thing in a long string of unresolved ethnocentric differences. It was simply the end result of piling too many bricks on a pressure-filled relationship.

Often, to justify putting off communication, we convince ourselves that a problem is "not a big deal." "I'll just forget about it," we say. Unfortunately, we *never* forget. Each time we get angry with someone and then say, "I'll forget about it," we take that irritation and store it away in an imaginary paper sack. As the irritations continue, our sack becomes full and then, one day when the sack is straining at it's seams and we have reached our boiling point, we will empty it. At the least appropriate time—during an argument—we will strategically employ the contents of our sack.

As an argument begins, out comes our imaginary paper sack. The irritations stored up in the sack become ammunition for our arguments. As we argue, we systematically and hurtfully empty our sack of issues and problems and irritations—like so many poison darts—until we have bludgeoned each other, sometimes to irreparable harm in our relationship.

The better way of handling our problems is to deal with them as they occur. We should communicate our feelings with those we think are offending us and avoid filling our imaginary sacks. We need to take the time to sit down and discuss our perceived problems—to clear the air and show our concern about the quality of our relationship.

Obviously, there are important guidelines to follow when setting up such a discussion. Some people have no problem with airing their concerns, but they have difficulty in disagreeing agreeably. That is, they lack the tact, respect, and spirit of compromise that is needed to successfully broach topics of concern.

With the help of my students over the years, I have assembled a list of the "Do's and Don'ts of Caring Communication." (See Appendix.) These are principles that we can all follow when we decide to air our differences.

America's ethnic, racial and cultural diversity, and the resulting ethnocentric differences, creates an opportunity for us to recognize and accept differing viewpoints. As we encounter a multiplicity of belief systems and begin to discuss those differences and negotiate our practices, we learn that there are many acceptable forms of behavior.

As we celebrate our uniqueness, we should also realize that our diversity often strains our relationships. If we truly appreciate the diversity of our workmates, schoolmates, roommates, teammates, spouses and other significant people, we should recognize the need to cultivate positive communication techniques. Let's not be satisfied by merely talking about good communication; let's challenge ourselves to do it. Only by caring, careful communication can we form lasting relationships and successfully tap the strength and resources inherent in a diverse America.

Though I have not seen Gazpacho or Franco since our high school days, I hope that they have learned, as I have, that the diversity they bring to relationships is not always understood as a good thing. Sometimes diversity is merely considered "different," and that difference is often seen as something bad or wrong. On the contrary though, diversity is what makes us rich and wonderful. A nation woven together as "*la canasta*," the basket: whole, unified, strong, complete, and ready to aspire to our greatest dreams together.

Chapter 9
The Diversity Movement

"Prize [people] who challenge the status quo and who embrace chaos. This diversity of thought and action will lead us all to greatness." ~ David Diaz

There was a serious air about the table as we discussed how we could change the employee demographics of our college to be more representative of the demographics of our state. I had not been at the college too long at that point, but I could tell that these discussions had taken place in the past—and they surely would again in the future. Everyone had been sitting for hours, generating plenty of heat, but little light. All the "heavy hitters" of the college were there—president, vice presidents, deans, directors and supervisors, as well as representatives from the faculty and staff groups. Given the hourly wage of the sum total of occupants in that room, I thought it ludicrous that we could sit and stare at each other for such a long period of time.

One of the subjects of discussion was how we should decide on a person's ethnicity and whether they meet the criteria for enhancing our ratio of ethnic minorities. I'm not sure what brought it out, but after an indeterminable period of silence someone finally broke the ice, looked in my direction and said, "Hey Dave, you just got hired here, what does it take to classify someone as 'Hispanic'?"

I glanced around the table—the air was thick with anticipation, a few chuckles could be heard and then . . . stillness. How should I respond to a question that I thought so nonsensical? I mean we hire people at a college because they are the best person for the job, I hoped. How can we be so detached in conversation and quibble over quotas as if we were counting sheep in a fit of insomnia?

What I wanted to say was, "*Pues hombre*, a better than average skill with duct-tape and spray paint," which would have been an answer befitting the seriousness of the question, in my opinion.

Instead, my White Tortilla training prevailed. After feigned consideration, I finally broke silence and said, "I'll have to get back to you on that one."

In its tumultuous 40-year history, affirmative action has yet to yield the "level playing field" that would signal its ultimate success. Given the lure of opportunity for promotions, salary increases, career advancement, school admissions, scholarships and financial aid, the fact that the numbers of "ethnic minorities" have swelled considerably is not surprising.

However, affirmative action has had only limited success in improving conditions for minorities within America. Too often, the benefits of affirmative action are doled out to those for whom it was never intended. As more and more people "qualify" for affirmative action relief, the *truly* disadvantaged serve as the stepping-stones over which the more "privileged minorities" traverse.

***

One of the problems that I have with the modern "diversity movement" is that it tends to oversimplify race and ethnicity—ostensibly for the purpose of categorization, education and/or research.

What defines race or ethnicity? Is it bloodlines, surname, generational status? I have perused the literature and found hundreds of studies using demographic surveys for educational research. There are typically no criteria for marking one racial or ethnic group over another.

Affirmative action "bean counters" (no pun intended) continue to keep track of the diversity within a population; yet, across studies or censuses, I am not sure that there is a universal definition of what it means to be included in an ethnic group or race.

When asked to identify race when completing the U.S. Census survey, a survey respondent can list as many as is deemed appropriate. The process typically allows for self-identification as the preferred means of obtaining information about an individual's race and ethnicity. It's no wonder the ranks of minorities have bloated to such vast proportions, given that people decide for themselves what ethnicity and race they possess. The need of the moment serves as the ultimate arbiter.

There seems to be no agreement within and among state and federal agencies on whether to consider race and ethnicity together or separately.[7] The federal government considers race and Hispanic origin to be two separate and distinct concepts.

For Census 2000, the question on Hispanic origin was asked directly before the question on race. The question asked respondents if they considered themselves "Spanish, Hispanic or Latino"; if they said yes to this question, they were asked to identify their origins (i.e., Cuban, Mexican, Puerto Rican, South or Central American, or other Spanish culture or origin). Regardless of ethnicity, the respondents could then select as many races as befit their requirements. So, an individual could be a Hispanic (ethnicity) who is "white" and "black" (race). And why not? Given the prevalence of interracial marriage in the United States—and the almost complete lack of criteria for ethnic and racial designation—it is small wonder that there is such ambiguity. Ethnic and racial selection can be based on which ethnic or racial group a person most identifies with and/or which group may serve his/her purpose in terms of placement or promotion.

It always bothers me when I hear a multicultural educator or writer make sweeping statements about ethnic beliefs and cultural practices because they often have not carefully considered the complexities. When we bear in mind that a "Hispanic" can be from any number of Spanish-speaking countries and can fall into more than one race category, I find it hard to believe that many, if any, broad generalizations can be made regarding "Hispanics/Latinos."

One must also consider the wide variations between people who hail from the same ethnic group and race but who fall into different subgroups. By subgroups I am referring to the distinctions between native transplanted, first-generation and second-generation Americans, and the myriad differences in the way each of these groups might manifest their ethnicity.

I would not dare to make generalizations about these subgroups except in my own instance. My grandma Minga was a native transplant (born in Mexico and migrated to the United States) who held stubbornly to almost every aspect of her native culture—from language and religion to food and customs. She chose to isolate herself and depend largely on her children to navigate societal obligations. My father, on the other hand, was first-generation American whose beliefs and customs were heavily influenced by the country and customs of his parents. However, his response to being first-generation was to divorce himself and his family as much as possible from the culture of his ancestors as a strategy for achieving success. This strategy deeply influenced his second-generation children, as I can attest. By adopting the ideals of my first-generation parents, however, I became educated enough to understand the underlying philosophical differences and made more conscious choices about my implementations of those beliefs. As a result, I am more prone to embracing the language and many of the customs of my ancestors without fear of failing to fully assimilate—with the caveat that I keep the primary lessons of the White Tortilla as an overall priority.

By the time the beliefs and cultural practices of the native transplant reach the third- and fourth-generation children, they have probably also reached their melting point and have been infused with any number of odds and ends of cultural practices and beliefs.

Given the subjectivity surrounding different races, ethnic groups and subgroups, I find it difficult to imagine how one could meaningfully categorize ethnicity or race, let alone make tidy statements about the ethnic beliefs and practices within any group, or subgroup.

I prefer the distinction that has been made by Richard Rodriguez, who simply states that, "America is becoming brown."[8] Interracial and interethnic marriages are continually rendering cultural distinctions and identities moot. The persistence of intermarriages between races and ethnic groups continually dilute cultural identities—religious practices, language, dietary and health practices—and wears away the relevance of ethnic typing. If America is truly becoming brown, it should be impossible to clearly quantify the origins of a people or distinguish between ethnic groups. Indeed, it may be irrelevant.

The "browning of America" means, thankfully, that we are starting to break down the barriers of differences of all kinds. It means that more and more people are successfully negotiating the challenges of the White Tortilla by assimilating into the majority, which is rapidly becoming brown.

Though many forms of discrimination have continued unabated throughout America, affirmative action was, and is currently, not the sole answer. Though modest benefits to the ratios of ethnic minorities may have been achieved, lasting positive change has not been forthcoming. The gains for women and blacks have probably surpassed those for other minorities, but even so, it's not enough.

At best, affirmative action has been a band-aid approach to sucking-chest-wound. Flaws in affirmative action have fostered reverse discrimination and quota systems—something that even proponents abhor.

Tolerance and breaking the cycle of discrimination must start with *individuals*. That is, each of us should practice the ideal of non-discrimination consistently and teach it to our children and others within our sphere of influence. Would such a practice merely equate to "pie-in-the-sky idealism? Perhaps, but attempting to encourage individual solutions to global problems is no more idealistic than attempts to legislate morality. Forty years of affirmative action legislation has proved this point, I think.

That's not to say that we shouldn't encourage reasonable legislation. However, if we attempt to obligatorily impose "equal opportunity" upon the public by forcing "equal results" (i.e., proportional hiring or admissions practices), we will end up alienating too many people. In the end, we will wind up creating situations that are as unfair as those they were designed to correct. In fact, they might be more unfair since they discriminate with purpose and intent rather than merely blind prejudice. Equal opportunity cannot be applied preferentially to one race, ethnicity or gender over another; otherwise it is not equal.

* * *

Obviously, intolerance of any kind must be resisted. We need to teach our children and our students to be aware of, and to tolerate, if not accept, all kinds of differences. To accomplish this, we must rethink our societal, organizational and operational structures. We must rewire personal relationships and typical organizational structures and we must minimize hierarchies until there are no operational distances between us.

For example, if there is no operational distance between a mid-level manager and a janitor, then the janitor's good idea for how to better serve the corporation's clients should be considered directly by the manager, with no intermediaries. The janitor should be welcomed to the manager's office, or better, the manager should come to the janitor's office! Wouldn't it be a refreshing change to remove the distance that typically exists because of different positions in life, to demolish barriers that are arbitrarily assigned due to a status structure within our society? Would embracing such "chaos" really be bad?

And that idea, offered in sincerity by the janitor should be acted on, because it is a good idea, not because it came from a janitor, or a part-time dishwasher, or one of the children in a school. We can still recognize the differences that make us distinct and define our jobs, but we should not allow those differences to create personal distance, aloofness, or status distinctions between us.

Educators should set an example in classrooms that consist of more than rhetoric or an occasional "critical thinking" assignment. We must show students how to deconstruct complex institutional relationships. Students should be able to challenge or argue respectfully with their teachers, and teachers with administrators and employees with employers—and that without fear of reprisal.

There is a cost to this type of process. The cost to those in power or authority is that of relinquishing their power to those in subordinate positions, thereby empowering them to excel.

In a classroom, this means allowing students a privileged and important role in the management of the learning process. Teachers need to learn to relinquish some of the control they exert in the classroom. Rather than simply acting as dispensers of knowledge, they should facilitate instructional practices that place more importance on the role of the student in constructing knowledge. Further, this process demands more active forms of classroom instruction that engage the student in the process of learning and that rely on student input for shaping instructional objectives.

The cost to those in subordinate positions is to respect their access privileges and to craft arguments and ideas toward the goal of making things better, fairer, truer and more just, for everyone, not just themselves or their private interest group.

The advantages of this type of empowerment greatly outweigh the costs. Empowered students, or employees are more mindful of the role they play in their own success and in the successes of those around them. They are more committed to positive change and, given the opportunity, will serve as prime movers in constructing a positive environment at work, in the classroom and in society at large.

The solutions to discrimination must begin with those who have the power, position and authority. Leaders in schools, colleges and businesses, tend to build up impenetrable hierarchies that serve as buffers between the elite and the non-elite, the majority and the minority, the light-skinned and dark-skinned.

This status may be used as a shield and/or a sword. People in positions of authority—politicians, teachers, cops, administrators, doctors, and others—often use their position to shield themselves from others who are different or who have different ideas about how things should be done. And if that doesn't work, they use their position as a sword to eliminate those who are different.

***

When I was in high school my father and mother hired a lawyer to defend one of my friends and me in a minor legal matter. We were guilty, which was beside the point, of course, but our alibi was sound. We won that case—providing yet another example of how justice can be blind *and* dumb, I think. And we were relieved, especially me, since punishment (from my parents) would probably have been cruel and unusual.

While standing outside the courthouse after the verdict, I was with my parents, a few of my friends and our lawyer. My dad did something that embarrassed me at the time. The backside of our lawyer's pants were full of dust—acquired from sitting at some desk and billing at $200 per hour, I'm sure—and my dad unabashedly walked up and swept away the dust, using his bare hand to brush off the lawyer's butt! I was completely embarrassed by his action. How could he stoop so low?

Several weeks passed, and I had the occasion to discuss the situation with my dad. Afterwards, I realized that by his action he was neither accepting a lower status, nor acknowledging a position of privilege of the lawyer, but instead he was showing there was no difference between them.

My dad gave that lawyer an opportunity to reassess their relationship as one of equals, of friends and *compadres*. In response, the lawyer, being somewhat flustered himself, grabbed my father's hand and shook it, while his other hand reached out and embraced my father about the shoulders—*compadres*.

Where there is a hierarchy, there are the powerful and the powerless, where the hierarchy has been deconstructed, there is familiarity, and everyone is empowered. In other words, an act of familiarity provides the opportunity for the acceptance (or rejection) of a new relationship, one that is more akin to family or friend than casual acquaintance.

In later years, I watched my father time and again display this maxim. He would try to bridge gaps between himself and others by serving others and breaking down the barriers to familiarity and intimacy.

It is not realistic, of course, to assume that we can become *compadres* with everyone, but we must at least provide that opportunity, especially those of us who are in a position of authority.

I have tried, imperfectly, to copy the practice of familiarity and to teach, by example, how we must reduce arbitrary hierarchies that exist between us. Some time ago, I accepted an opportunity for my family to feed the homeless as a way of graphically demonstrating a flattened hierarchy. I didn't want us to just pay for the food, but to prepare it and serve it too (I figured it was too easy to throw money at this situation and less personal). So, we purchased the food, got up at 4:00 am to cook it, delivered it, and served it. All my children participated from the oldest (22 yrs) to the youngest (2 yrs). Two of them—Valerie and Christina—were living out of town and traveled a great distance to be there. I was proud of their actions. We served those people and talked with them and laughed with them and, for a few hours anyway, there were no differences between us.

I wanted my children to understand that homeless people are neither above us nor below us in their need for independence, respect, self-esteem, or dignity and we must not allow socioeconomic status to determine our relationships.

My youngest daughter walked to the tables and handed carnations to those sitting there, and I saw more than one tear shed. Tears of gratitude perhaps, tears of empowerment and privilege I hope.

***

At this point in my career, I am an administrator as well as an educator. In both roles, I try to flatten operational distance by appreciating diversity and by fostering familiarity.

As an administrator, my goal is to stay focused on my "role" not on my "position." Too often it is convenient to use our position of authority to create a zone of comfort and control. It is easy to shut out others, or overrule them, and to run things as we please. Often, those in authority only promote or hire those who are like-minded—those who will conform to the status quo.

As I understand it, my role is to serve others: students, faculty, staff and administrators. I try to allow the people I serve to challenge the status quo, to not only embrace change, but embrace chaos if need be. It is a goal each year to help each of the people that I serve to achieve success in their endeavors for the college. In effect, their success determines my success.

In implementing this philosophy, sufficient leeway is given to those who have important ideas, or who are early adopters of innovations. I try to stay out of their way, or better, provide them what they need to excel in their jobs. There is no need to fear change or new and different ideas. Instead, I try to actively involve all those who must live with the results and empower them to achieve their finest work.

How can we achieve better ethnic diversity in our workplaces? I hope that by now you understand that I believe we don't need to artificially enhance diversity—America is becoming brown, all by itself. However, we need to rise up as *individuals* to celebrate diversity, acknowledge it, empower it and allow it to lead us into the future by removing barriers to access and familiarity. We need to insist on changes that are fair to all of us, not just groups: white, black, hispanic, or asian, but to all individuals, regardless of our race, ethnicity or color.

Chapter 10
Lessons of the White Tortilla

"Nothing worth having comes without some kind of fight; got to kick at the darkness till it bleeds daylight." ~ Bruce Cockburn

There are four critical lessons that I have tried to share in this book. These lessons are the defining characteristics of The White Tortilla and comprise the basic teachings that I have grown up with and that I have taught my family.

First, to achieve success, it is important to assimilate into the dominant culture. By my parent's definition, one that I believe in and have tried to articulate in this volume, assimilation means distinguishing ourselves by outstanding performance in all that we attempt.

There are three primary thrusts of assimilation to be pursued by the White Tortilla: (1) pursuit of a comprehensive and well-rounded education, while being active and participative during the time doing so, (2) pursuit of a mastery of the English language, insofar as it is the dominant and/or necessary language of a country, and, (3) adaptation to the cultural traits of those around us. The latter point does not imply relinquishing ones cultural practices, but simply means reassessing cultural practices in the light of how they might affect other people and being ready to modify them out of a desire to demonstrate a spirit of compromise and respect for others.

Second, as we encounter the myriad ethnocentric differences that often affect our relationships negatively, we should remember to cultivate and practice caring communication techniques. Caring communication allows us to recognize that there are many different viewpoints and behaviors that are appropriate. Regularly practicing good communication techniques can reward us with the ability to compromise and to disagree agreeably.

Third, to promote tolerance and to embrace cultural, racial and ethnic diversity, it is important to reduce operational distance by avoiding, or deconstructing, artificial hierarchies that separate people. Implementing this axiom involves serving others, without respect to position or privilege, and providing them the opportunity to become *compadres*—friends and co-conspirators on the road to success, happiness and health. These important traits should be encouraged, nourished, and practiced by all people, but especially people in positions of power and authority.

As affirmative action attests, it is often counterproductive to attempt to force equal opportunity by governmental, organizational or institutional fiat. This type of reform must start at the *individual* level—forwarded by progressive, like-minded and committed people who will serve as role models in this respect.

Fourth, we should establish a priority of giving to others—making a difference in the lives of others by contributing to their needs in some meaningful way. Not just giving to friends and family members, but also to others within our sphere of influence.

We must be constantly on the lookout for opportunities to give. Each of us has a "sphere of influence," an environment that we live, work and play in. Each day we come in contact with the same people—people with needs and who might benefit from our time, interest, expertise or money. The opportunities lie directly before us, we need only to reach out and grasp the significance and act on it.

My father lived only 59 years and yet he has had a profound affect on my life and the lives of others. My mother, 88 years[9] at the time of this writing, has also influenced my thinking and actions deeply. I have always listened to their advice; indeed, they have taught me that there is no good reason not to: advice is free, a gift from one person to another. Worst case (or perhaps best case), there is nothing to compel us to accept that advice and, thus, no reason to be threatened by it. Without a doubt, advice—especially when offered by someone who loves and cares for us—may just help us to achieve the goals we desire.

My advice, to my children and to others who may read this book, is to heed the lessons of The White Tortilla. They have been tried and tested by my parents and by me and have withstood both scrutiny and time. These principles have made a lasting, beneficial difference in countless lives.

As one White Tortilla to another, I can only wish you the best in your attempts to achieve your dreams in this life and to make positive contributions to others within your sphere of influence. I urge you to remain steadfast in pursuing your dreams and enriching the lives of all those with whom you come in contact.

End Notes

1. "Pachuco" refers to a Mexican-American youth who belongs to a neighborhood gang and wears showy clothing that identifies him with a particular group.
2. When I got to 5th grade, one of my more educated classmates instructed me that the reason that Christopher Columbus called my Mexican ancestors "Indians" (*los Indios*) was because he got lost looking for India. I suppose we were lucky he wasn't looking for the Canary Islands, the Virgin Islands, or Turkey.
3. The Philosophy of Movimiento Estudiantil Chicano de Aztlán. M.E.Ch.A. Philosophy Papers – Amended. Retrieved May 5, 2004 from the Internet:
   http://www.angelfire.com/sd/MEChAde SDSU/AmendedPhilosophyPapers.html
4. Though not grammatically correct, the conjunction "mi'jo" is the commonly pronounced variant of "mi hijo"—my son.
5. History of Mexican Courtship and Wedding Customs. Retrieved May 5, 2004 from the Internet:
   http://www.indiansun.net/mex_wed.htm
6. Jose, N. (1987). The silent gift: A project for spiritual health. Journal of School

Health, 57(2), 72–73. The assignment that I use in my classes has been adapted from the article above.

7. Grieco, E. M., & Cassidy, R. C. (March 2001). Overview of race and Hispanic origin 2000: Census 2000 Brief. U.S. Census Bureau. Retrieved May 6, 2004 from the Internet: http://www.census.gov/prod/2001pubs/c2kbr01-1.pdf

8. Rodriguez, R. (2002). Brown: The Last Discovery of America. New York, NY: Viking Penguin.

9. In February of 2004 my mother wrote: "I don't feel well, I'm ready to go . . . I've had a long life, loved my children, my grandchildren and my great-grandchildren. You all know I loved you dearly." My mother passed away on May 30, 2004, just two days before the first printing of this book went to printer. She had been very excited about the book though, unfortunately, she never got to read it. I decided not to rewrite any portions of the book.

Do's and Don'ts of Caring Communication

Listed below are the "Do's and Don'ts of Caring Communication." There are probably many more than those mentioned here. Perhaps you can add to this list by discussing it with a friend.

When Discussing Problems DO . . .

1. Pick a time when you will not be interrupted or rushed.
2. Remove distractions (e.g., unplug or turn off phone, TV, radio, stereo, etc.).
3. Try to stay calm and be aware of the loudness and pitch of your voice.
4. Listen to what is being said.
5. Be prepared with solutions.
6. Be prepared to compromise: remember that your way is one way, not the only way.
7. Respect the other person's point of view. Disagree agreeably.
8. Explain why certain things bother you.
9. Say something positive about the other person.
10. Limit your complaint to the most important things and clearly identify the problem from your viewpoint.

When Discussing Problems DON'T . . .

1. Bring up old problems (i.e., those from your imaginary paper sack).
2. Blame the situation on other person.
3. Be patronizing or sarcastic.
4. "Gang up" by bringing in a 3rd party to the conversation.
5. Interrupt the other person when they are talking.
6. Delay discussion too long.
7. Confront the person when you are still upset.
8. Swear.
9. Assume that they understand your point of view—ask them to review what you have said.
10. Assume you understand what they have said—repeat your understanding and ask if it is correct.

Chapter Discussion Questions

Chapter 1- The White Tortilla

- After reading the book, how would you describe a 'White Tortilla'? What are the positive and negative aspects of being a White Tortilla? How would you minimize the negative aspects?
- The term "beaner" has been used as a derogatory way of referring to Mexicans. Why do you think David (from his 10-year-old vantage point in the book) referred to Butchie as a 'beaner'?
- Do you think Butchie's experience might have been different? If yes, under what circumstances? If no, why not?
- What is David's definition of assimilation? How does this definition differ from more common definitions? What do you think are the benefits and drawbacks of assimilation?
- What are the key elements of David's description of 'true diversity?'

Chapter 2- A "Good Education"

- Though David described his experience negatively, do you think there were important positive results in his attending Catholic school?
- Though David and his parents each prized (valued) a 'good education,' what are the similarities and differences in the conditions that shaped their respective values?
- According to David, what are the advantages of students "involving themselves fully in the experience" of a good education?
- Do you put forth the same effort in all your classes or in all aspects of your job? If so, what makes you apply such effort equally?" If not, what explains your unequal efforts? In either case, do your practices in this regard affect your health either positively or negatively?

Chapter 3- Finding a "Good Job"

- How did David's dad and mom defy their parents' Mexican cultural traditions?
- What were the similarities/differences between how David and his father experienced race/ethnicity in the U.S.?
- Do you think that those experiences would have been different had they lived in Mexico? Why? Why not?
- List several instances of prejudice and discrimination experienced by David's family.

- According to David, what makes a job a "good job?" What do you consider to be a "good job?" List some of the characteristics of a job that you would aspire to. What major goals do you need to accomplish before you could attain your dream job?
- According to David, what is a major issue with young people and their work ethic in the U.S.? Do you agree or disagree?
- According to David, there is a positive correlation between success in attaining a good education and success in finding a good job. Do you agree? Why? Why not?

Chapter 4- The Language of Success
- David's parents did not speak to their children in Spanish in the home. Why?
- What do you think are the benefits of monolingualism? What are the drawbacks?
- What were some of David's unique experiences with language/communication and how has he dealt with them?
- Describe Dave's beliefs regarding bilingual education.

Chapter 5- The Church of My Youth
- How did Catholicism shape David's worldview? How has religion shaped your values, positively or negatively? How does religion shape the values of

others that share your cultural background?

- What role does religion play in spiritual health? Can one be spiritually healthy without being religious?

Chapter 6- La Comida Mexicana

- Explain Dave's grandmother's use of home remedies. Can you think of any folk medicine remedies from your family history?
- Explain the importance of food to cultural identity providing examples from this chapter.
- What meals did you enjoy in your youth and what meals do you think are representative of your cultural background?
- Do you remember ever changing your habits to fit in with the practices of a different culture? Has anyone you know ever done so? Site examples and expand your thoughts and feelings about the event.

Chapter 7- Give Until it Hurts

- What is the major lesson of the "Saturday Rocket Races?"
- What is giving selflessly? Can you describe a time when you exhibited any of this characteristic when giving? Describe how it made you feel and what you think were the benefits.
- When does giving become negative?
- Explain the concept of the "Silent Gift".

Chapter 8- Ethnocentric Differences

- Do you remember assigning nicknames to your friends and/or acquaintances? What were the nicknames and why did you give them these names? Do you think these nicknames represented a "put down?" Why? Why not?
- Is alcohol consumption an accepted practice in your home? Did you or your friends ever exhibit "drinking game" behavior? What are your thoughts on this practice now? Positive? Negative?
- David described an ethnocentric difference between him and his college roommate ("sharp knives in the soapy dishwater"). Describe a problem(s) that you have faced with a friend or acquaintance that was reducible to an ethnocentric difference. What was the outcome?
- Review the "Do's and Don't of Caring Communication" (Appendix). Can you relate a situation where you used any of these recommendations, or failed to use them when you should have?

Chapter 9- The Diversity Movement

- Describe the diversity movement according to David.
- How does one qualify race and/or ethnicity?
- What is a Latino? Describe the wide range of diversity among Latinos.

- How might one make a generalization regarding Latinos without stereotyping?

Chapter 10- Lessons of the White Tortilla
- What are the four critical lessons of the White Tortilla? Which of these lessons are most important to you?

Topical Discussion Questions

Culture
- Define culture.
- What are the values and norms that you feel are indicative of your culture?
- Where are your parents from? Where are your grandparents and great grandparents from?
- What generation American are you?
- What holidays, traditions, or foods do you celebrate? How are they important to your identity?
- What unique qualities and characteristics do you possess from your upbringing?

Race/Ethnicity
- What is race? What is ethnicity?
- If you could change your skin color, would you? Why? Why not?
- What, if anything, does a person's race tell us about an individual?
- What was your most memorable encounter with someone from another culture/race?

Immigration
- What are your thoughts regarding immigration to the U.S.?
- Does immigration benefit the U.S.?

- What are drawbacks of immigration?
- How do you personally benefit from immigrants coming to the U.S.?
- What is your family's immigration story?

Education
- Do you believe there is a direct correlation between educational attainment and success? Are there other factors that may limit someone's ability to succeed in U.S. society?
- Is success determined only by individual effort?
- What kind of policy or program would you devise to ensure equal access to higher education? What about equal access to the job market?
- Do you think a teacher's background, such as gender, culture, race, and personal beliefs, affect their teaching style? Why? Why not?
- Do you think learning from an ethnic minority teacher would benefit a person's education? If so, how? If not, why not?

Prejudice & Discrimination
- Define prejudice and discrimination.
- Can one be prejudiced and not discriminate?
- Describe a time you experienced prejudice or discrimination?
- Does a society have the responsibility to provide equity for all its members?

Diversity

- How do you define diversity?
- What role do you believe groups like M.E.Ch.A. (Movimiento Estudiantil de Aztlán) play in promoting diversity and education on college campuses?
- How would you promote diversity in your community or on your campus?

About the Author

David P. Diaz was born and raised in Oxnard, California. He is an educator and administrator, and the author of numerous articles in the discipline of educational pedagogy and technology. David earned his doctoral degree in Education from Nova Southeastern University. He resides in California with his wife, son, and youngest daughter. The White Tortilla is his first book.